Bible Study Workbook for Women

Grow Closer to God with Guided Reflections, Scripture Prompts, and Weekly Devotionals for Everyday Life

Welcome Aboard, Check Out This Limited-Time Free Bonus!

Ahoy, reader! Welcome to the Ahoy Publications family, and thanks for snagging a copy of this book! Since you've chosen to join us on this journey, we'd like to offer you something special.

Check out the link below for a FREE e-book filled with delightful facts about American History.

But that's not all - you'll also have access to our exclusive email list with even more free e-books and insider knowledge. Well, what are ye waiting for? Click the link below to join and set sail toward exciting adventures in American History.

Access your bonus here
https://ahoypublications.com/
Or, Scan the QR code!

Table of Contents

Dedication

To the seekers, the journeyers, and all who long to know God more intimately. May these pages be a humble guide, drawing you closer to the heart of the One who faithfully walks with you every step of the way.

Introduction

Welcome to a year-long journey designed to deepen your understanding of God and empower you to live a life fully aligned with His purposes.

Over the next 52 weeks, we will embark on an intentional exploration of faith, divided into four distinct quarters, each focusing on a vital aspect of our walk with God.

Our path begins by **Knowing God Deeper** (Quarter 1), where we will intimately explore His unchanging attributes and character. From there, we will transition into **Living Out Our Faith** (Quarter 2), delving into the practical ways our beliefs shape our daily actions and choices. The third quarter, **Connecting with Others** (Quarter 3), will guide us in building healthy relationships. Finally, we will conclude with **Living with Purpose** (Quarter 4), discovering and embracing God's unique calling for our lives.

Each week offers a focused theme, relevant Scripture passages for meditation, guided reflection questions, a devotional thought, and a prayer prompt.

Also, each week ends with **a workbook section** where you can document your thoughts and insights.

May this book be a faithful companion, a catalyst for spiritual growth, and a source of profound encouragement as you draw closer to the heart of God.

1. Setting the Foundation
(Weeks 1-2)

Week 1: Welcome and Your Journey with God

Take a deep breath.

In the midst of your busy life, you've chosen to carve out this sacred space to connect more deeply with the heart of God. This workbook is a year-long exploration of Scripture, thoughtful reflection, and intentional growth in your relationship with the One who loves you most.

Think of this book as a trusted companion on your faith walk. Each week, we'll gently unpack Biblical truths, ask questions that stir your heart, and offer daily bread for your soul. Our aim is simple yet profound: to help you grow closer to God, not through striving, but through a deeper understanding of His Word and its application to your everyday life.

Your Unique Path

Every woman's journey with God is unique, filled with its own joys, challenges, and moments of profound connection. Whether you've walked with Him for many years or are just beginning to explore His love, this workbook welcomes you exactly where you are. There's no expectation of perfection, only an invitation to be open and honest with yourself and with God.

Take a moment now to quiet your heart and consider:

What has your journey with God looked like so far?

_____

_____

_____

What are some significant moments or experiences that come to mind?

_____

_____

_____

What are your deepest longings for your relationship with God right now?

_____

_____

_____

What does "growing closer" look and feel like to you?

_____

_____

_____

What hopes do you have as you begin this year-long study?

_____

_____

_____

Scripture Prompt:

Spend some time meditating on **Psalm 139:23-24**:

> *"Search me, O God, and know my heart! Try me and know my thoughts! And see if there be any grievous way in me, and lead me in the way everlasting!"* (ESV))

What words or phrases in this psalm resonate with you today?

_____

_____

_____

What does it mean for God to search your heart?

_____

_____

_____

How does this desire for God's searching relate to your own desire to grow closer to Him?

_____

_____

_____

Guided Reflection:

Use a notebook to jot down your thoughts and responses to the questions we unpacked and your reflections on Psalm 139:23-24. Be honest and allow yourself to be vulnerable. This is a conversation between you and God.

Weekly Devotional: The Importance of Consistent Connection

Finding consistent time for what truly matters can feel like a constant battle. Yet, just as regular nourishment sustains our physical bodies, consistent connection with God through His Word and prayer nourishes our souls. It's in these intentional moments that we learn to recognize His voice, understand His character, and experience the depth of His love.

This weekly devotional, along with the daily Scripture readings and reflection prompts, is designed to be a gentle rhythm in your week. It's about creating space for your spirit to breathe and be filled.

As you commit to this year-long journey, remember that even small, consistent steps can lead to growth. Be patient with yourself, celebrate the small victories, and trust that God will meet you in the quiet moments of study and reflection.

Prayer Prompt:

Take a few moments to pray about your journey ahead. Ask God to open your heart and mind to His Word, to reveal Himself to you in new ways, and to guide you as you seek to grow closer to Him.

Personal Reflection & Growth Journal

Significant Moments / Insights from This Week's Study

What happened? What was the insight?

Emotional/Spiritual Responses:

Spiritual Insights/Lessons Learned:

- First thoughts:

- New perspectives gained:

_____

_____

_____

_____

- My Response/Action:

_____

_____

_____

_____

What helped me connect with God/grow this ?week?

_____

_____

_____

_____

What hindered my connection/?growth?

_____

_____

_____

_____

Week 2: The Power and Purpose of God's Word

Stepping into Scripture

Last week, we began by acknowledging our individual journeys and our desire for deeper connection with God. This week, we turn our attention to the very tool God has given us to know Him intimately: His Word, the Bible.

The Bible is living and active (Hebrews 4:12), a divine tapestry woven with threads of history, poetry, prophecy, and personal encounters with God. It reveals His character, His promises, His plan for humanity, and His unfailing love for you.

Think about your current relationship with the Bible:

- How often do you engage with Scripture? What does that engagement typically look like?

- What are some of your perceptions or feelings about reading the Bible? Do you find it encouraging, challenging, confusing, comforting?

- What do you hope to gain from studying the Bible more intentionally this year?

Scripture Prompt:

Reflect on **2 Timothy 3:16-17**:

> *"All Scripture is breathed out by God and profitable for teaching, for reproof, for correction, and for training in righteousness, that the man of God may be complete, equipped for every good work."* (ESV))

What does it mean to you that Scripture is "breathed out by God"? What are the different ways this passage says Scripture is "profitable"? How does engaging with Scripture equip you for "every good work?"

Guided Reflection:

Use your notebook to record your thoughts on the questions above and your reflections on 2 Timothy 3:16-17. Consider any past experiences with Scripture that have been particularly meaningful or challenging.

Weekly Devotional: Engaging with Scripture for Transformation

Simply reading the Bible is a good start, but true growth comes when we engage with it actively and intentionally. This means not just reading words but seeking to understand their meaning within their historical and literary context, reflecting on how they apply to our lives, and allowing them to shape our thoughts, attitudes, and actions.

Throughout this workbook, you'll be encouraged to go beyond surface-level reading through the daily prompts and weekly reflections. These are designed to help you:

- **Understand:** What does this passage truly mean?
- **Reflect:** How does this truth relate to my life and experiences?
- **Apply:** What practical steps can I take based on what I've learned?

This active engagement is key to transformation. As we consistently immerse ourselves in God's Word and allow it to speak to our hearts, we will indeed grow closer to Him and become more equipped for the life He has called us to live.

Prayer Prompt:

Pray that God would give you a hunger for His Word and the wisdom to understand it. Ask Him to open your eyes to the truths He wants to reveal to you this year and to help you apply them to your daily life.

Personal Reflection & Growth Journal

Significant Moments / Insights from This Week's Study

What happened? What was the insight?

_____

_____

_____

_____

_____

Emotional/Spiritual Responses:

_____

_____

_____

_____

Spiritual Insights/Lessons Learned:

- First thoughts:

_____

_____

_____

_____

- New perspectives gained:

_____

_____

_____

_____

- My Response/Action:

_____

_____

_____

_____

What helped me connect with God/grow this ?week?

_____

_____

_____

_____

What hindered my connection/?growth?

_____

_____

_____

_____

I. Quarter 1: Knowing God Deeper (Weeks 3-15) -
Theme: Exploring God's Attributes

Week 3: God Our Creator

Let's start at the very beginning, focusing on God as our Creator. The opening words of Scripture start with, "In the beginning, God..." (Genesis 1:1). This foundational truth shapes everything we understand about ourselves, our world, and our relationship with Him.

Think for a moment about the sheer wonder of creation. From the smallest seed that bursts forth with life to the vast expanse of the cosmos, everything bears the imprint of God's power, wisdom, and artistry.

Consider these aspects of God as Creator:

- What comes to mind when you think about God creating the universe? What emotions or thoughts does it evoke?
- In what ways do you see God's creativity reflected in the world around you today? Consider both the grand scale and the intricate details.
- How does the knowledge that God created you personally (Psalm 139:13-16) impact how you view yourself?

Scripture Prompt:

Meditate on **Genesis 1:1**:

> *"In the beginning, God created the heavens and the earth."* (ESV)

What is the significance of the very first words of the Bible? What does this statement tell us about God's priority and power? How does this foundational truth influence your understanding of everything else in Scripture?

Now, also read **Psalm 19:1**:

> *"The heavens declare the glory of God, and the sky above proclaims his handiwork."* (ESV))

How does the natural world serve as a testament to God's glory? What aspects of creation specifically point to His "handiwork"?

Guided Reflection:

Use a notebook or journal to record your reflections on the questions above and your insights from Genesis 1:1 and Psalm 19:1. Pay attention to any new perspectives or deeper understandings that emerge as you ponder God's role as Creator.

Weekly Devotional: Finding God in the Created World

Sometimes, in our pursuit of God, we focus solely on the written Word or specific spiritual practices. While these are vital, we can also encounter God in the beauty and order of the world He has made. The intricate patterns of a flower, the breathtaking vista of a mountain range, the delicate balance of an ecosystem all whisper of His power and design.

Taking time to observe creation can be an act of worship.

It allows us to see glimpses of God's character: His creativity, His attention to detail, His boundless power, and His inherent beauty. As you go about your week, try to be more intentional about noticing the wonders around you. In these moments, you can connect with the Creator through His creation.

Prayer Prompt:

Spend time in prayer thanking God for His creation. Ask Him to open your eyes to see His handiwork in new ways and to deepen your appreciation for His power and artistry.

Personal Reflection & Growth Journal

Significant Moments / Insights from This Week's Study

What happened? What was the insight?

_____

_____

_____

_____

_____

Emotional/Spiritual Responses:

_____

_____

_____

_____

Spiritual Insights/Lessons Learned:

- First thoughts:

_____

_____

_____

- New perspectives gained:

_____

_____

_____

- My Response/Action:

_____

_____

_____

_____

What helped me connect with God/grow this ?week?

_____

_____

_____

_____

What hindered my connection/?growth?

_____

_____

_____

_____

Week 4: God's Unfailing Love

We now turn to one of the most comforting and foundational truths about our Heavenly Creator: His unfailing love. This isn't a fleeting emotion or a conditional affection; it is a deep, steadfast, and unwavering commitment to us.

Think about the times in your life when you have felt deeply loved. What did that feel like? Now, try to grasp the magnitude of a love that is even greater, a love that never gives up, never fails, and is offered freely and abundantly by the Creator of the universe.

Reflect on these aspects of God's unfailing love:

- How does the idea of God's unfailing love differ from human love that can sometimes waver or end? What comfort does this bring you?

- Can you recall a time when you particularly felt God's love for you? What circumstances surrounded that experience?

- How does understanding God's love impact the way you view yourself and your worth?

Scripture Prompt:

Spend time meditating on **Romans 5:8**:

> *"but God shows his love for us in that while we were still sinners, Christ died for us."* (ESV)

What does it mean that God showed His love for us *while we were still sinners*? What does this reveal about the nature of His love? How does the sacrifice of Christ demonstrate the depth of this love?

Now, also read **1 John 4:8**:

> *"Anyone who does not love does not know God, because God is love."* (ESV)

How does this verse define God's very essence? What does it imply about everything He does? How should this understanding shape our own capacity for love?

Guided Reflection:

Use a notebook or your journal to record your reflections on the questions above and your insights from Romans 5:8 and 1 John 4:8. Allow yourself to truly absorb the profound truth of God's love for you.

Weekly Devotional: Resting in God's Affection

In a world that often demands performance and measures worth by achievement, the unconditional love of God stands as a powerful anchor. We don't have to earn it, strive for it, or be perfect to receive it. It is freely given, a gift born out of His very nature.

This week, focus on resting in God's love. Take moments throughout your day to remind yourself that you are deeply loved by the Creator of the universe. Allow this truth to wash over you, bringing comfort, security, and a sense of belonging.

Consider how this unfailing love can transform the way you interact with yourself and others. When we are secure in God's love, we are freer to extend grace, forgive imperfections (both our own and others'), and live with a greater sense of peace and joy.

Prayer Prompt:

Spend time in prayer thanking God for His unfailing love. Ask Him to help you truly grasp the depth and breadth of His affection for you and to empower you to live in the light of that love.

Personal Reflection & Growth Journal

Significant Moments / Insights from This Week's Study

What happened? What was the insight?

_____

_____

_____

_____

_____

Emotional/Spiritual Responses:

_____

_____

_____

_____

Spiritual Insights/Lessons Learned:

- First thoughts:

_____

_____

_____

- New perspectives gained:

_____

_____

_____

- My Response/Action:

_____

_____

_____

_____

What helped me connect with God/grow this ?week?

_____

_____

_____

_____

_____

What hindered my connection/?growth?

_____

_____

_____

_____

_____

Week 5: God's Perfect Holiness

After reflecting on God's love, we now turn to another crucial aspect of His character: His perfect holiness. While His love draws us near, His holiness reminds us of His complete otherness, His absolute purity, and His separation from all that is sinful or imperfect. Understanding God's holiness helps us grasp the depth of His righteousness and the seriousness of sin.

Take a moment to consider what the word "holy" means to you. What images or ideas come to mind? It's more than just being "good"; it speaks of a complete and utter perfection, a moral purity beyond our full comprehension.

Reflect on these aspects of God's perfect holiness:

- How does the concept of God's holiness make you feel? Does it inspire awe, reverence, or perhaps even a sense of distance? Why?
- In what ways does God's holiness contrast with the imperfections and sinfulness we see in the world and in ourselves?
- How does understanding God's holiness deepen your appreciation for His grace and mercy?

Scripture Prompt:

Spend time meditating on **Leviticus 19:2**:

"You shall be holy, for I the Lord your God am holy." (ESV))

What does it mean that God commands us to be holy because He is holy? Is this a call to perfection? How can we, as imperfect beings, strive for holiness?

Now, also read **Isaiah 6:3**:

"And one called to another and said: 'Holy, holy, holy is the Lord of hosts; the whole earth is full of his glory!'" (ESV))

What is the significance of the repetition of "holy" three times? What does it emphasize about God's character? How does the vision of God's holiness in this passage impact your understanding of His majesty?

Guided Reflection:

Use your notebook or journal to record your reflections on the questions above and your insights from Leviticus 19:2 and Isaiah 6:3. Be honest about any challenges or questions you have regarding God's holiness.

Weekly Devotional: Approaching a Holy God

The perfect holiness of God can sometimes feel intimidating. How can we, with our flaws and failings, draw near to someone so utterly pure? The answer lies in God's own provision: through the sacrifice of Jesus Christ, we are made righteous in His sight. It is through His Son that we can approach the holy God with confidence and without fear of condemnation.

Understanding God's holiness should not drive us away but rather inspire a deeper reverence and a greater appreciation for the gift of grace. It reminds us of the seriousness of sin and the immense cost of our redemption. As we grow in our understanding of God's holiness, may it lead us to a greater desire for purity in our own lives, not out of obligation, but out of a longing to honor the One who is altogether holy.

Prayer Prompt:

Spend time in prayer acknowledging God's perfect holiness. Thank Him for the way He has made it possible for you to draw near to Him through Christ. Ask for His help in growing in holiness in your own life, reflecting His purity in your thoughts, words, and actions.

Personal Reflection & Growth Journal

Significant Moments / Insights from This Week's Study

What happened? What was the insight?

_____

_____

_____

_____

_____

Emotional/Spiritual Responses:

_____

_____

_____

_____

Spiritual Insights/Lessons Learned:

- First thoughts:

_____

_____

_____

- New perspectives gained:

_____

_____

_____

- My Response/Action:

_____

_____

_____

_____

What helped me connect with God/grow this ?week?

_____

_____

_____

_____

What hindered my connection/?growth?

_____

_____

_____

_____

Week 6: God's Abundant Grace

Having contemplated God's perfect holiness, we now turn to His abundant grace. Grace is often defined as God's unmerited favor: His loving-kindness and mercy freely given, not because we deserve it, but because of His generous nature. It is the very essence of how He interacts with us, especially considering our imperfections.

Think about times in your life when you received unexpected kindness or help. How did that make you feel? God's grace is infinitely more profound, a constant outpouring of His goodness towards us.

Reflect on these aspects of God's abundant grace:

- What does the phrase "unmerited favor" truly mean to you in the context of your relationship with God?
- Can you identify specific instances in your life where you have experienced God's grace, even when you felt undeserving?
- How does understanding God's grace free you from feelings of guilt, shame, or the need to constantly earn His approval?

Scripture Prompt:

Spend time meditating on **Ephesians 2:8-9**:

> *"For by grace you have been saved through faith. And this is not your own doing; it is the gift of God, not a result of works, so that no one may boast."* (ESV))

What does this passage tell us about how salvation is received? What role does grace play? Why is it emphasized that salvation is "not your own doing" or "a result of works"?

Now, also read **Titus 3:5**:

> *"he saved us, not because of works done by us in righteousness, but according to his own mercy, by the washing of regeneration and renewal of the Holy Spirit,"* (ESV)

How does this verse further emphasize that our salvation is based on God's mercy rather than our own good deeds? What is the significance of "regeneration and renewal of the Holy Spirit" in the context of His grace?

Guided Reflection:

Use your notebook or journal to record your reflections on the questions above and your insights from Ephesians 2:8-9 and Titus 3:5. Consider how the truth of God's grace impacts your understanding of your worth and your relationship with Him.

Weekly Devotional: Living in the Light of Grace

The abundant grace of God is not just a one-time gift at the moment of salvation; it is the very atmosphere in which we live as believers. It fuels our growth, forgives our failures, and empowers us to live in a way that honors Him.

When we truly understand and embrace God's grace, it transforms our perspective. We move from a place of striving and fear to a place of rest and confidence in His love. We become more willing to extend grace to others, knowing how freely it has been given to us.

This week, let's consciously choose to live in the light of God's grace. Release any burdens of guilt or the need for self-justification. Embrace the freedom that comes from knowing you are loved and accepted, not because of what you've done, but because of who God is.

Prayer Prompt:

Spend time in prayer thanking God for His abundant grace. Ask Him to help you fully receive and live in the reality of His unmerited favor. Pray for the ability to extend that same grace to those around you.

Personal Reflection & Growth Journal

Significant Moments / Insights from This Week's Study

What happened? What was the insight?

_____

_____

_____

_____

_____

Emotional/Spiritual Responses:

_____

_____

_____

_____

_____

Spiritual Insights/Lessons Learned:

- First thoughts:

_____

_____

_____

_____

- New perspectives gained:

_____

_____

_____

_____

- My Response/Action:

_____

_____

_____

_____

What helped me connect with God/grow this ?week?

_____

_____

_____

_____

What hindered my connection/?growth?

_____

_____

_____

_____

Week 7: God's Unchanging Faithfulness

The unchanging faithfulness of God provides a solid anchor for our souls. His promises are true, His love endures, and His commitment to us never wavers, regardless of our circumstances or feelings. This steadfastness is a cornerstone of our trust in Him.

Think about the things in your life that have been unreliable or have let you down. Now, contrast that with the character of God, who is consistently true to His Word and His nature.

Reflect on these aspects of God's unchanging faithfulness:

- What does it mean to you that God's faithfulness is *unchanging*? How does this provide security and hope in your life?

- Can you recall a time when you experienced God's faithfulness in a tangible way, perhaps during a difficult season?

- How does knowing that God is always faithful impact your own commitment and loyalty in your relationships and to Him?

Scripture Prompt:

Spend time meditating on **Lamentations 3:22-23**:

"The steadfast love of the Lord never ceases; his mercies never come to an end; they are new every morning; great is your faithfulness." (ESV)

What does this passage emphasize about the consistency and renewal of God's love and mercies? What does it mean that His faithfulness is "great" and "new every morning"? How can this truth sustain you through challenging times?

Now, also read **Hebrews 13:8**:

"Jesus Christ is the same yesterday and today and forever." (ESV)

How does the unchanging nature of Jesus Christ reflect the unchanging faithfulness of God? What comfort do you find in this constant presence and character of Christ?

Guided Reflection:

Use your notebook or journal to record your reflections on the questions above and your insights from Lamentations 3:22-23 and Hebrews 13:8. Consider specific areas of your life where you need to rely on God's unwavering faithfulness.

Weekly Devotional: Trusting in God's Promises

Because God is unchangingly faithful, we can have complete confidence in His promises. Throughout Scripture, He has declared His love, His provision, His guidance, and His eternal presence with us. When life feels uncertain and the ground beneath us seems to shift, we can stand firm on the solid rock of His Word.

This week let's focus on identifying and claiming God's promises for our lives. As you read Scripture, pay attention to the declarations He makes about His character and His intentions toward His children. Remind yourself that He is not a God who lies or changes His mind (Numbers 23:19). His faithfulness extends to every generation.

By anchoring ourselves in God's promises, we cultivate a deeper trust and resilience in the face of life's storms. We learn to lean not on our own understanding or fleeting circumstances, but on the One whose faithfulness endures forever.

Prayer Prompt:

Spend time in prayer thanking God for His unchanging faithfulness. Ask Him to bring specific promises from His Word to your mind and heart. Pray for the grace to trust in these promises, especially when circumstances seem contrary.

Personal Reflection & Growth Journal

Significant Moments / Insights from This Week's Study

What happened? What was the insight?

_____

_____

_____

_____

_____

Emotional/Spiritual Responses:

_____

_____

_____

_____

Spiritual Insights/Lessons Learned:
- First thoughts:

_____

_____

_____

- New perspectives gained:

_____

_____

_____

_____

- My Response/Action:

_____

_____

_____

_____

What helped me connect with God/grow this ?week?

_____

_____

_____

_____

What hindered my connection/?growth?

_____

_____

_____

_____

Week 8: God's All-Knowing Wisdom

Life often presents us with complex situations, difficult decisions, and paths that aren't always clear. Yet, we serve a God whose understanding is infinite, whose wisdom encompasses all things. He sees the beginning from the end, knows every detail, and possesses perfect insight into every circumstance. This all-knowing wisdom is a profound comfort and a guide for our lives.

Consider the times you've sought guidance or understanding. Reflect on the limitations of human knowledge and the peace that comes from trusting a source of perfect wisdom.

Reflect on these aspects of God's all-knowing wisdom:

- How does the knowledge that God knows everything about you – your thoughts, your past, your future – make you feel? Does it bring comfort or unease? Why?
- Can you recall a time when you sought God's wisdom in a challenging situation? How did He guide you?
- How does trusting in God's wisdom differ from relying solely on your own understanding or the advice of others?

Scripture Prompt:

Spend time meditating on **Proverbs 3:5-6**:

"Trust in the Lord with all your heart, and do not lean on your own understanding. In all your ways acknowledge him, and he will make straight your paths." (ESV)

What does it mean to "not lean on your own understanding"? What does it look like to "acknowledge him in all your ways"? What is the promise that follows this trust and acknowledgement?

Now, also read **Romans 11:33**:

"Oh, the depth of the riches and wisdom and knowledge of God! How unsearchable are his judgments and how inscrutable his ways!" (ESV)

What does this exclamation convey about the extent of God's wisdom and knowledge? How does the idea that His judgments are "unsearchable" and His ways "inscrutable" impact your perspective on trying to fully understand God?

Guided Reflection:

Use your notebook or journal to write down your reflections on the questions above and your insights from Proverbs 3:5-6 and Romans 11:33. Consider areas in your life where you need to release your own understanding and trust in God's wisdom.

Weekly Devotional: Leaning on Divine Understanding

Human wisdom is limited and often influenced by our emotions, experiences, and biases. God's wisdom, however, is pure, objective, and sees the complete picture. When we face decisions or uncertainties, seeking His perspective through prayer and His Word offers guidance that surpasses our own understanding.

This week let's practice intentionally seeking God's wisdom in our daily lives. Before making a decision, big or small, take a moment to pray and ask for His guidance. As you read Scripture, look for principles and truths that can illuminate your path. Remember that trusting in God's wisdom doesn't always mean we'll understand everything, but it does mean we can have confidence that His way is best.

Cultivating a posture of humility, acknowledging our limitations, and consistently turning to God for insight will deepen our reliance on His all-knowing mind and lead us on paths that are ultimately for our good and His glory.

Prayer Prompt:

Spend time in prayer asking God for His wisdom and discernment in specific areas of your life where you need guidance. Pray for a humble heart that is willing to follow His leading, even when it doesn't align with your own initial thoughts.

Personal Reflection & Growth Journal

Significant Moments / Insights from This Week's Study

What happened? What was the insight?

_____

_____

_____

_____

_____

Emotional/Spiritual Responses:

_____

_____

_____

_____

_____

Spiritual Insights/Lessons Learned:

- First thoughts:

_____

_____

_____

_____

- New perspectives gained:

_____

_____

_____

_____

- My Response/Action:

_____

_____

_____

_____

What helped me connect with God/grow this ?week?

_____

_____

_____

_____

What hindered my connection/?growth?

_____

_____

_____

_____

Week 9: God's Everywhere Presence

We navigate days filled with various locations, tasks, and interactions. Yet, one constant remains for the believer: the unwavering presence of God. Scripture assures us that He is not distant or confined but is with us wherever we go. This truth of God's omnipresence offers immense comfort and security.

Consider moments when you have felt alone or isolated. Reflect on the reassurance that comes from knowing God is always near, even when unseen.

Reflect on these aspects of God's everywhere presence:

- How does the understanding that God is always with you impact your feelings of loneliness or fear?

- In what everyday situations can you consciously recognize God's presence around you?

- How does the knowledge of God's omnipresence influence the way you behave and make choices, knowing He is always aware?

Scripture Prompt:

Spend time meditating on **Psalm 139:7-12**:

> *"Where shall I go from your Spirit? Or where shall I flee from your presence? If I ascend to heaven, you are there! If I make my bed in Sheol, you are there! If I take the wings of the morning and dwell in the uttermost parts of the sea, even there your hand shall lead me, and your right hand shall hold me fast. If I say, "Surely the darkness shall cover me, and the light about me be night," even the darkness is not dark to you; the night is bright as the day, for darkness is as light with you."* (ESV)

What feelings or thoughts arise as you read this powerful description of God's omnipresence? What comfort do you find in the truth that there is nowhere you can go to escape His presence? How does the imagery of darkness and light relate to His awareness of you?

Now, also read **Acts 17:28**:

> *"for 'In him we live and move and have our being'; as even some of your own poets have said, 'For we are indeed his offspring.'"* (ESV)

What does it mean to live, move, and have our being "in him"? How does this verse emphasize the intimate and constant connection we have with God?

Guided Reflection:

Use your notebook or journal to record your reflections on the questions above and your insights from Psalm 139:7-12 and Acts 17:28. Consider specific times and places where you can intentionally acknowledge God's nearness this week.

Weekly Devotional: Walking with God Throughout the Day

The reality of God's omnipresence transforms our daily routines. Knowing He is always near means we never truly face any moment alone. Whether we are at work, with family, running errands, or in quiet solitude, His presence surrounds us, offering comfort, guidance, and companionship.

This week let's cultivate an awareness of God's nearness in the ordinary moments of our days. Speak to Him as you go about your tasks. Acknowledge His presence in the beauty you see, the challenges you face, and the interactions you have. Remember that prayer is not confined to specific times or places; it can be a continuous conversation with the God who is always with you.

By consciously recognizing His omnipresence, we move from simply believing He is everywhere to experiencing His nearness in a tangible way. This awareness fosters a deeper sense of connection and allows us to walk through each day with the constant assurance of His love and support.

Prayer Prompt:

Spend time in prayer thanking God for His constant presence in your life. Ask for a greater awareness of His nearness throughout your day and for the comfort and guidance that comes from knowing He is always with you.

Personal Reflection & Growth Journal

Significant Moments / Insights from This Week's Study

What happened? What was the insight?

_____

_____

_____

_____

_____

Emotional/Spiritual Responses:

_____

_____

_____

_____

Spiritual Insights/Lessons Learned:

- First thoughts:

_____

_____

_____

_____

- New perspectives gained:

_____

_____

_____

_____

- My Response/Action:

_____

_____

_____

_____

What helped me connect with God/grow this ?week?

_____

_____

_____

_____

What hindered my connection/?growth?

_____

_____

_____

_____

Week 10: God's Ultimate Power

As we continue to explore the depths of God's character, we encounter His ultimate power. He is not limited or constrained; His strength and authority are absolute. He spoke the universe into existence, and His power sustains all things. Understanding this attribute brings us a sense of security and hope, knowing that nothing is beyond His control.

Consider situations in your life that feel overwhelming or impossible. Reflect on the comfort that comes from knowing there is a God whose power surpasses all limitations.

Reflect on these aspects of God's ultimate power:

- When you think about God's power, what images or events from Scripture come to mind? (e.g., creation, miracles, resurrection)
- How does knowing that God has ultimate power impact your fears and anxieties?
- In what areas of your life do you need to trust more fully in God's power to work?

Scripture Prompt:

Spend time meditating on **Psalm 62:11**:

"Once God has spoken; twice have I heard this: that power belongs to God," (ESV)

What is the significance of the repetition in this verse? What is the clear declaration being made about power? How does this singular truth shape your understanding of the world and your place in it?

Now, also read **Matthew 19:26**:

"But Jesus looked at them and said, "With man this is impossible, but with God all things are possible."" (ESV)

In what context was Jesus speaking these words? How does this statement about God's possibility relate to the challenges you face? What does it mean to live with the understanding that "all things are possible" with God?

Guided Reflection:

Use your notebook or journal to write down your reflections on the questions above and your insights from Psalm 62:11 and Matthew 19:26. Consider specific challenges you are facing and how trusting in God's ultimate power can shift your perspective.

Weekly Devotional: Relying on God's Strength

Our own strength and resources are often limited. We encounter obstacles that seem insurmountable and face situations where we feel powerless. It is in these moments that the reality of God's ultimate power becomes our greatest hope. He is not only capable but willing to intervene and work on our behalf.

This week let's consciously choose to rely on God's strength rather than our own. Bring your weaknesses and limitations before Him, trusting that His power is made perfect in our weakness (2 Corinthians 12:9). Remember that the same power that raised Jesus from the dead is available to those who believe.

By acknowledging our need for His strength and actively seeking His help, we open ourselves to experience His power in tangible ways. This doesn't always mean our circumstances will change as we desire, but it does mean we can face them with a supernatural strength and a confident hope in the One who holds all power in His hands.

Prayer Prompt:

Spend time in prayer acknowledging God's ultimate power and sovereignty. Bring before Him any situations where you feel powerless or overwhelmed. Ask for His strength to sustain you and His power to work in and through those circumstances.

Personal Reflection & Growth Journal

Significant Moments / Insights from This Week's Study

What happened? What was the insight?

_____

_____

_____

_____

_____

Emotional/Spiritual Responses:

_____

_____

_____

_____

_____

Spiritual Insights/Lessons Learned:
- First thoughts:

_____

_____

_____

_____

- New perspectives gained:

_____

_____

_____

_____

- My Response/Action:

_____

_____

_____

_____

What helped me connect with God/grow this ?week?

_____

_____

_____

_____

What hindered my connection/?growth?

_____

_____

_____

_____

Week 11: God's Perfect Justice

We live in a world where injustice often prevails, where the innocent suffer and the guilty sometimes go unpunished. In contrast to this, God's perfect justice is a comforting assurance. He is righteous and fair in all His judgments. His justice is not driven by emotion or bias but by His perfect understanding of truth and righteousness.

Consider times you have witnessed or experienced injustice. Reflect on the longing for true fairness and the comfort that God's perfect justice offers.

Reflect on these aspects of God's perfect justice:

- How does the knowledge of God's perfect justice bring you comfort in a world filled with unfairness?
- In what ways does God's justice differ from human justice systems? What are the limitations of human judgment?
- How does understanding God's justice influence your own approach to fairness and your response to injustice around you?

Scripture Prompt:

Spend time meditating on **Psalm 89:14**:

"Righteousness and justice are the foundation of your throne; steadfast love and faithfulness go before you." (ESV)

What does it mean that righteousness and justice are the "foundation" of God's throne? How do His steadfast love and faithfulness relate to His justice? What does this tell you about the nature of God's rule?

Now, also read **Romans 12:19**:

"Beloved, never avenge yourselves, but leave it to the wrath of God, for it is written, "Vengeance is mine, I will repay, says the Lord."" (ESV)

Why are we instructed not to seek our own revenge? What does this passage reveal about God's role in administering justice? How does trusting in His justice bring freedom from bitterness and the need for personal retribution?

Guided Reflection:

Write down your reflections on the questions above and your insights from Psalm 89:14 and Romans 12:19. Consider any situations where you need to release the desire for personal vengeance and trust in God's perfect justice.

Weekly Devotional: Trusting in God's Righteousness

Because God's justice is perfect, we can trust that ultimately, all things will be made right. This doesn't always mean we will see justice unfold according to our timing or understanding, but it assures us that God's righteousness will prevail. He sees every wrong, knows every motive, and will ultimately judge with perfect fairness.

This week let's focus on cultivating a deep trust in God's righteousness. When we witness or experience injustice, let us remember that He is the ultimate judge. This doesn't excuse us from seeking justice in our own spheres of influence, but it frees us from the burden of carrying anger and resentment.

By trusting in God's perfect justice, we can find peace knowing that He is in control and that His way is ultimately right. We can release the need for immediate resolution and rest in the assurance that His justice will prevail in His perfect time.

Prayer Prompt:

Spend time in prayer acknowledging God's perfect justice and righteousness. Bring before Him any situations where you long for justice. Ask for His peace and the ability to trust in His timing and His ways. Pray for wisdom in how to respond to injustice in a way that honors Him.

Personal Reflection & Growth Journal

Significant Moments / Insights from This Week's Study

What happened? What was the insight?

_____

_____

_____

_____

_____

Emotional/Spiritual Responses:

_____

_____

_____

_____

_____

Spiritual Insights/Lessons Learned:

- First thoughts:

_____

_____

_____

_____

- New perspectives gained:

_____

_____

_____

_____

- My Response/Action:

_____

_____

_____

_____

What helped me connect with God/grow this ?week?

_____

_____

_____

_____

What hindered my connection/?growth?

_____

_____

_____

_____

Week 12: God's Tender Mercy

While God's holiness reveals the seriousness of sin and His justice ensures fairness, His tender mercy is the compassionate outpouring of His love towards those who are hurting, broken, and in need. It is His willingness to forgive, to comfort, and to extend grace in the face of our failures and weaknesses.

Think about times when you have needed compassion or forgiveness. Reflect on the relief and comfort that mercy brings. God's mercy is far greater and more tender than any we can imagine.

Reflect on these aspects of God's tender mercy:

- How does the idea of God's tender mercy resonate with your own experiences of needing forgiveness or comfort?

- In what ways do you see God's mercy extended in the world around you, both in your own life and in the lives of others?

- How does receiving God's tender mercy influence your ability to show mercy and compassion to those around you?

Scripture Prompt:

Spend time meditating on **Psalm 103:8**:

"The Lord is merciful and gracious, slow to anger and abounding in steadfast love." (ESV)

What do the words "merciful" and "gracious" convey about God's character in this verse? What does it mean that He is "slow to anger" and "abounding in steadfast love"? How does this description offer you comfort and assurance?

Now, also read **Ephesians 2:4-5**:

"But God, being rich in mercy, because of the great love with which he loved us, even when we were dead in our trespasses, made us alive together with Christ—by grace you have been saved" (ESV)

What does it mean that God is "rich in mercy"? How did His mercy manifest itself towards us "even when we were dead in our trespasses"? How does this connect with the concept of salvation by grace?

Guided Reflection:

Write down your answers on the questions above and your insights from Psalm 103:8 and Ephesians 2:4-5. Consider specific areas where you need to receive God's tender mercy or extend it to others.

Weekly Devotional: Receiving and Giving Mercy

God's tender mercy is a gift freely given, and as recipients of this grace, we are called to extend the same compassion to those around us. Just as He meets us in our brokenness with understanding and forgiveness, we are to approach others with gentleness and empathy.

This week let's be intentional about both receiving and giving mercy. Allow yourself to be embraced by God's tender care, acknowledging your own need for His grace. At the same time, look for opportunities to show compassion to those who are struggling, offering a listening ear, a helping hand, or a word of encouragement.

By embracing God's mercy and extending it to others, we reflect His character and become instruments of His love in the world. This reciprocal flow of mercy fosters healing, understanding, and deeper connection within our communities and with God.

Prayer Prompt:

Spend time in prayer thanking God for His tender mercy in your life. Ask for a greater awareness of His compassion and for a heart that is more readily able to extend that same mercy to others, especially those who may be difficult to love or forgive.

Personal Reflection & Growth Journal

Significant Moments / Insights from This Week's Study

What happened? What was the insight?

_____

_____

_____

_____

_____

Emotional/Spiritual Responses:

_____

_____

_____

_____

Spiritual Insights/Lessons Learned:

- First thoughts:

_____

_____

_____

_____

- New perspectives gained:

_____

_____

_____

_____

- My Response/Action:

_____

_____

_____

_____

What helped me connect with God/grow this ?week?

_____

_____

_____

_____

What hindered my connection/?growth?

_____

_____

_____

_____

Week 13: Review and Reflection on Knowing God

The Lord is
my shepherd;
I shall not want.
PSALM 23:1

We've journeyed through a rich landscape of God's character over the past eleven weeks, exploring His roles as Creator, His unfailing love, perfect holiness, abundant grace, unchanging faithfulness, all-knowing wisdom, everywhere presence, ultimate power, perfect justice, and tender mercy. This week is set aside to pause, reflect, and allow these truths to settle more deeply into our hearts.

Think back over the attributes we've studied. What has resonated with you most? What challenged your understanding? How has your perception of God grown or shifted during this time?

Scripture Prompt:

Spend time meditating on **James 4:8**:

> *"Draw near to God, and he will draw near to you."* (ESV)

In what ways have you felt God drawing near to you as you've studied His attributes? What steps can you take to continue drawing near to Him?

Guided Reflection:

Reflect on the attributes of God explored in Weeks 3 through 12. Consider the following questions:

- Which attribute of God surprised you the most or gave you a new perspective?

- How has understanding God's [choose one or two specific attributes] impacted your daily life or your relationship with Him?

- What is one thing you want to remember or apply from this quarter's study of God's character?

- In what ways do you sense a desire to know God even more deeply as a result of this study?

Devotional: Continuing to Seek Deeper Knowledge of God

Our exploration of God's attributes this quarter is not an endpoint but rather a step further on a lifelong journey of knowing Him. The more we learn about who He is, the more we understand His love for us and His purposes for our lives.

Continue to cultivate a curiosity about God. Remain open to learning and growing in your understanding of His multifaceted character. Engage with Scripture with a desire to see Him more clearly. Talk to Him in prayer about what you are learning and how it impacts you.

The desire to know God more intimately is a holy pursuit. May the insights gained in these past weeks fuel a continued passion to seek His face and to grow in your relationship with the One who is all-encompassing and eternally worthy of our adoration.

Prayer Prompt:

Spend time in prayer thanking God for revealing more of Himself to you during this quarter. Ask for a continued hunger to know Him more deeply and for His guidance as you continue your study in the weeks ahead.

Personal Reflection & Growth Journal

Significant Moments / Insights from This Week's Study

What happened? What was the insight?

_____

_____

_____

_____

Emotional/Spiritual Responses:

_____

_____

_____

_____

Spiritual Insights/Lessons Learned:

- First thoughts:

_____

_____

_____

- New perspectives gained:

_____

_____

_____

- My Response/Action:

_____

_____

_____

_____

What helped me connect with God/grow this ?week?

_____

_____

_____

_____

What hindered my connection/?growth?

_____

_____

_____

_____

Week 14: From Knowing to Living: Bridging Understanding and Action

The foundation we've laid in understanding who God is will now inform how we live out our faith in the everyday rhythms of our lives.

Think about how a deeper understanding of God's love, grace, and faithfulness, for example, might influence your interactions with others or your approach to challenges. The knowledge we've gained is not meant to remain abstract; it is intended to shape our actions and attitudes.

Scripture Prompt:

Spend time meditating on **Philippians 3:10**:

> *"that I may know him and the power of his resurrection, and may share his sufferings, becoming like him in his death,"* (ESV)

Notice Paul's desire here. It goes beyond intellectual knowledge to a deeper, experiential knowing of Christ, including the power of His resurrection and even a sharing in His sufferings. How does this verse challenge your own pursuit of knowing God? How might a deeper knowing of Him empower you to live differently?

Guided Reflection:

Reflect on the connection between knowing God and living out your faith. Consider the following questions:

- How do you anticipate the attributes of God we studied in Quarter 1 influencing the way you live your life?

- What is one area of your daily life where you would like to see your understanding of God make a tangible difference?

- As you look ahead to the theme of "Living Out Our Faith," what are your hopes for practical growth and application?

Devotional: Moving Forward in Our Faith Journey

Our faith is not meant to be stagnant; it is a dynamic journey of growth and application. The insights we've gained about God's character provide the "why" behind how we live. Now, as we transition into Quarter 2, we will begin to explore the "how": how we can practically embody our faith in our relationships, our decisions, and our daily routines.

This transition is an opportunity to connect the theological truths we've studied with the practical realities of our lives. May the knowledge of God's deep love compel us to love others more fully. May the experience of His grace empower us to extend grace. May the assurance of His faithfulness give us courage in uncertain times.

As we move forward, let us do so with open hearts and a willingness to allow our understanding of God to transform the way we live.

Prayer Prompt:

Spend time in prayer asking God to help you connect the knowledge you've gained about Him with the practical living out of your faith. Pray for wisdom and guidance as you begin to explore the theme of "Living Out Our Faith" in the next quarter.

Personal Reflection & Growth Journal

Significant Moments / Insights from This Week's Study

What happened? What was the insight?

_____

_____

_____

_____

_____

Emotional/Spiritual Responses:

_____

_____

_____

_____

Spiritual Insights/Lessons Learned:

- First thoughts:

_____

_____

_____

- New perspectives gained:

_____

_____

_____

- My Response/Action:

_____

_____

_____

_____

What helped me connect with God/grow this ?week?

_____

_____

_____

_____

What hindered my connection/?growth?

_____

_____

_____

_____

Week 15: Living Out Our Faith

Having spent the initial weeks deepening our understanding of God's character, we now turn our focus to how this knowledge practically shapes our lives. Our beliefs are not meant to be confined to our minds or hearts; they are intended to permeate every aspect of our existence, influencing our actions, our relationships, and our responses to the world around us.

Think about the connection between what you believe to be true and how you live each day. Does your outward life consistently reflect the truths you hold dear? This quarter will be an invitation to more intentionally align our actions with our faith.

Scripture Prompt:

Spend time meditating on **James 2:17**:

"So also faith by itself, if it does not have works, is dead."
(ESV)

What does this verse emphasize about the relationship between faith and action? What does it mean for faith to be "dead" if it doesn't have works? How does this challenge our understanding of what it means to truly believe?

Guided Reflection:

Reflect on the theme of "Living Out Our Faith." Consider the following questions:

- What does "living out your faith" look like in your current season of life?

- What is one area where you feel a gap between what you believe and how you act?

- As we begin this quarter, what is one practical step you hope to take in living out your faith more intentionally?

Devotional: Setting Our Hearts on Practical Application

The truths we've learned about God – His love, His justice, His mercy – are not just abstract concepts; they are the very principles that should guide our interactions and decisions. This quarter, we will delve into practical ways to embody these attributes in our daily lives. We will explore themes such as love in action, forgiveness, patience, humility, and integrity.

Our aim is not to create a list of rules but to cultivate a heart that naturally reflects God's character in all we do. As we engage with Scripture and reflection prompts focused on practical application, may we grow in our ability to live out our faith authentically and impactfully.

Let us approach this quarter with a willingness to examine our lives and to allow God's Word to shape not just what we know, but how we live.

Prayer Prompt:

Spend time in prayer asking God to guide you as you explore the practical aspects of living out your faith. Pray for a heart that is eager to apply His truths to your daily life and for the strength to act in ways that honor Him.

Personal Reflection & Growth Journal

Significant Moments / Insights from This Week's Study

What happened? What was the insight?

_____

_____

_____

_____

_____

Emotional/Spiritual Responses:

_____

_____

_____

_____

Spiritual Insights/Lessons Learned:

- First thoughts:

_____

_____

_____

- New perspectives gained:

_____

_____

_____

- My Response/Action:

_____

_____

_____

_____

What helped me connect with God/grow this ?week?

_____

_____

_____

_____

_____

What hindered my connection/?growth?

_____

_____

_____

_____

II. Quarter 2: Living Out Our Faith (Weeks 16-28) - Theme: Practical Application in Daily Life

Week 16: Love and Kindness in Action

Having set our hearts on living out our faith, we begin by exploring the foundational principles of love and kindness. These are not merely feelings but active choices that demonstrate the heart of God to those around us. Scripture consistently emphasizes the importance of loving God and loving our neighbor as ourselves (Matthew 22:37-39). Kindness is love put into action, extending grace and care in tangible ways.

Think about the times you have experienced genuine love and kindness from others. How did it impact you? Now consider how you can intentionally extend that same care to those in your sphere of influence.

Scripture Prompt:

Spend time meditating on **1 Corinthians 13:4-7**:

> *"Love is patient and kind; love does not envy or boast; it is not arrogant or rude. It does not insist on its own way; it is not irritable or resentful; it does not rejoice at wrongdoing, but rejoices with the truth. Love bears all things, believes all things, hopes all things, endures all things."* (ESV)

Reflect on each characteristic of love described in this passage. Which of these qualities comes most naturally to you? Which do you find most challenging to embody consistently? How can you intentionally grow in demonstrating these aspects of love through your actions?

Now, also read **Galatians 5:22**:

> *"But the fruit of the Spirit is love, joy, peace, patience, kindness, goodness, faithfulness, gentleness, self-control; against such things there is no law."* (ESV)

Notice that kindness is listed as a fruit of the Spirit. What does this imply about the source of true kindness? How can you cultivate a life that is more yielded to the Holy Spirit, allowing this fruit to grow and be expressed through you?

Guided Reflection:

Write down your thoughts on the questions above and your insights from 1 Corinthians 13:4-7 and Galatians 5:22. Consider specific individuals in your life, such as family, friends, colleagues, and neighbors, and brainstorm practical ways you can show them love and kindness this week.

Devotional: Showing God's Heart Through Our Actions

Our words can express love, but our actions often speak even louder. When we intentionally choose to be patient, kind, and generous, we reflect the very nature of God to those around us. These acts of love and kindness can open doors for deeper connection and can be powerful testimonies to the transformative power of the Gospel.

This week let's be mindful of opportunities to demonstrate love and kindness in tangible ways. This might involve offering a helping hand, listening attentively, speaking encouraging words, performing a small act of service, or simply extending patience and understanding in a challenging situation.

Remember that even small acts of love and kindness, done with a sincere heart, can have a significant impact. As we intentionally choose to love and be kind, we not only bless others but also deepen our own connection with the God who is the ultimate source of love.

Prayer Prompt:

Spend time in prayer asking God to fill you with His love and to give you eyes to see opportunities to show kindness to others. Pray for a willing heart and the strength to act in ways that reflect His love in your daily interactions.

Personal Reflection & Growth Journal

Significant Moments / Insights from This Week's Study

What happened? What was the insight?

_____

_____

_____

_____

_____

Emotional/Spiritual Responses:

_____

_____

_____

_____

Spiritual Insights/Lessons Learned:

- First thoughts:

_____

_____

_____

_____

- New perspectives gained:

_____
_____
_____
_____

- My Response/Action:

_____
_____
_____
_____

What helped me connect with God/grow this ?week?

_____
_____
_____
_____

What hindered my connection/?growth?

_____
_____
_____
_____

Week 17: Forgiveness and Reconciliation

Relationships are a beautiful and essential part of life, yet they are also often the places where hurt and offense can occur. Holding onto bitterness and unforgiveness can weigh us down and hinder our connection with God and others. Forgiveness, though sometimes difficult, is a powerful act of obedience and a pathway to healing and reconciliation.

Think about any relationships in your life where there has been hurt or brokenness. Reflect on the impact of holding onto unforgiveness and the potential for freedom that forgiveness can bring.

Scripture Prompt:

Spend time meditating on **Matthew 6:14-15**:

> *"For if you forgive others their trespasses, your heavenly Father will also forgive you, but if you do not forgive others their trespasses, neither will your Father forgive your trespasses."* (ESV)

What is the direct connection Jesus makes between our forgiveness of others and God's forgiveness of us? How does this emphasize the importance of extending forgiveness? What might be the implications of holding onto unforgiveness in our relationship with God?

Now, also read **Colossians 3:13**:

> *"bearing with one another and, if one has a complaint against another, forgiving each other; as the Lord has forgiven you, so you also must forgive."* (ESV)

What does it mean to "bear with one another"? What is the motivation for forgiving others according to this verse? How does reflecting on God's forgiveness of us empower us to forgive others?

Guided Reflection:

Write down your thoughts on the questions above and your insights from Matthew 6:14-15 and Colossians 3:13. Consider any specific individuals you may need to forgive or situations where reconciliation is needed. What steps might you need to take towards forgiveness and healing?

Devotional: The Healing Power of Letting Go

Forgiveness is not about condoning wrong behavior or forgetting the hurt that was caused. Instead, it is a conscious decision to release the bitterness, resentment, and the desire for revenge that can consume us. It is an act of obedience to God and a gift we give ourselves, freeing us from the emotional bondage of the past.

Reconciliation, where possible and healthy, is the beautiful outcome of forgiveness – the restoration of broken relationships. It requires humility, vulnerability, and a willingness from all parties involved. While reconciliation may not always be possible, forgiveness is always a choice we can make.

This week let's prayerfully consider any areas in our lives where forgiveness is needed. Ask God for the courage and grace to release those who have hurt us, trusting that He is the ultimate source of justice and healing. Where appropriate, seek opportunities for reconciliation, approaching those relationships with humility and a spirit of love.

Prayer Prompt:

Spend time in prayer asking God to reveal any areas of unforgiveness in your heart. Pray for the strength and willingness to forgive those who have hurt you, just as Christ has forgiven you. If there are opportunities for reconciliation, pray for wisdom and guidance in approaching those situations.

Personal Reflection & Growth Journal

Significant Moments / Insights from This Week's Study

What happened? What was the insight?

_____

_____

_____

_____

Emotional/Spiritual Responses:

_____

_____

_____

_____

Spiritual Insights/Lessons Learned:

- First thoughts:

_____

_____

_____

_____

- New perspectives gained:

_____

_____

_____

_____

- My Response/Action:

_____

_____

_____

_____

What helped me connect with God/grow this ?week?

_____

_____

_____

_____

What hindered my connection/?growth?

_____

_____

_____

_____

_____

_____

_____

_____

Week 18: Patience and Perseverance

Life is rarely a sprint; more often, it's a marathon filled with delays, obstacles, and moments that test our resolve. In these times, patience and perseverance are vital aspects of living out our faith. Patience allows us to wait with hope and a calm spirit, while perseverance empowers us to keep moving forward despite difficulties.

Think about situations in your life that require waiting or where you've faced significant challenges. Reflect on your natural response to these circumstances and the role that patience and perseverance have played.

Scripture Prompt:

Spend time meditating on **Romans 5:3-5**:

> *"Not only that, but we rejoice in our sufferings, knowing that suffering produces endurance, and endurance produces character, and character produces hope, and hope does not put us to shame, because God's love has been poured into our hearts through the Holy Spirit who has been given to us."* (ESV)

Notice the progression described in this passage. How does suffering, though difficult, ultimately lead to hope through endurance and character? What role does God's love, poured into our hearts, play in sustaining our perseverance?

Now, also read **Hebrews 12:1**:

> *"Therefore, since we are surrounded by so great a cloud of witnesses, let us also lay aside every weight, and sin which clings so closely, and let us run with endurance the race that is set before us,"* (ESV)

What imagery is used here to describe the Christian life? What does it mean to "lay aside every weight and sin"? What is the attitude with which we are called to run this "race"?

Guided Reflection:

Write down your thoughts on the questions above and your insights from Romans 5:3-5 and Hebrews 12:1. Consider specific areas where you are currently being called to exercise patience or where you need strength to persevere through challenges.

Devotional: Staying the Course with Hope

Patience is not passive resignation; it is an active waiting with expectation and trust in God's timing. It involves choosing a spirit of peace and contentment even when circumstances are not unfolding as we desire. Perseverance, on the other hand, is the steadfast determination to continue following God and pursuing His purposes, even when the path is difficult or unclear.

This week let's intentionally cultivate both patience and perseverance in our lives. When faced with delays or frustrations, let us pray for a calm and trusting heart. When confronted with obstacles, let us draw strength from God and remember the ultimate hope we have in Him.

Remember that growth often happens during seasons of waiting and through the challenges we overcome. By embracing patience and persevering in faith, we develop spiritual resilience and a deeper reliance on God's strength and timing.

Prayer Prompt:

Spend time in prayer asking God to cultivate patience within you, especially in areas where you tend to become frustrated or discouraged. Pray for the strength and determination to persevere through any challenges you are currently facing, keeping your eyes fixed on Him and the hope He provides.

Personal Reflection & Growth Journal

Significant Moments / Insights from This Week's Study

What happened? What was the insight?

_____

_____

_____

_____

_____

Emotional/Spiritual Responses:

_____

_____

_____

_____

_____

Spiritual Insights/Lessons Learned:

- First thoughts:

_____

_____

_____

_____

- New perspectives gained:

_____

_____

_____

_____

- My Response/Action:

_____

_____

_____

_____

What helped me connect with God/grow this ?week?

_____

_____

_____

_____

What hindered my connection/?growth?

_____

_____

_____

_____

Week 19: Humility and Service

Humility and service are two sides of the same coin in the Kingdom of God. Humility is recognizing our dependence on God and valuing others above ourselves, while service is the practical outworking of that humility, putting the needs of others before our own. Jesus Himself exemplified both perfectly, coming not to be served but to serve (Mark 10:45).

Think about individuals you admire for their humility and their servant hearts. Reflect on the impact of their attitude and actions. How can you cultivate these qualities more intentionally in your own life?

Scripture Prompt:

Spend time meditating on **Philippians 2:3-4**:

"Do nothing from selfish ambition or conceit, but in humility count others more significant than yourselves. Let each of you look not only to his own interests, but also to the interests of others." (ESV)

What does it mean to "count others more significant than yourselves"? How does this contrast with selfish ambition and conceit? What practical steps can you take to look not only to your own interests but also to the interests of others?

Now, also read **Mark 10:45**:

"For even the Son of Man came not to be served but to serve, and to give his life as a ransom for many." (ESV)

How does Jesus' own example shape our understanding of true leadership and greatness? What does it mean to "serve" in the context of our daily lives and relationships? How can we reflect Jesus' servant heart?

Guided Reflection:

Meditate on the questions above and your insights from Philippians 2:3-4 and Mark 10:45. Consider specific relationships or contexts where you can intentionally practice humility and service this week.

Devotional: Following the Example of Christ

True greatness in God's eyes is often found in humility and a willingness to serve. When we lay aside our pride and self-seeking desires, we create space for God to work through us and for us to genuinely connect with and uplift others. Service, done with a humble heart, is an act of love that reflects the character of Christ.

This week let's be intentional about seeking opportunities to serve those around us, whether in small, unseen ways or in more visible acts of kindness. This might involve offering help without expecting anything in return, listening attentively to someone in need, or using your gifts and talents to benefit others.

By embracing humility and cultivating a servant heart, we not only follow the example of Jesus but also experience the joy and fulfillment that comes from putting others first. This way of living transforms our relationships and allows God's love to flow through us more freely.

Prayer Prompt:

Spend time in prayer asking God to cultivate humility within you and to give you a heart that is eager to serve others. Pray for opportunities to put the needs of others before your own and for a spirit of genuine love and selflessness in your interactions.

Personal Reflection & Growth Journal

Significant Moments / Insights from This Week's Study

What happened? What was the insight?

_____
_____
_____
_____
_____

Emotional/Spiritual Responses:

_____
_____
_____
_____
_____

Spiritual Insights/Lessons Learned:

- First thoughts:

_____
_____
_____
_____

- New perspectives gained:

_____
_____
_____
_____

- My Response/Action:

_____

_____

_____

_____

What helped me connect with God/grow this ?week?

_____

_____

_____

_____

What hindered my connection/?growth?

_____

_____

_____

_____

Week 20: Integrity and Honesty

Integrity and honesty are the cornerstones of a life that honors God and builds trust with others. Integrity means living in alignment with our values and beliefs, even when no one is watching. Honesty is speaking the truth, even when it's difficult or uncomfortable. These qualities reflect God's own character and are essential for authentic Christian living.

Think about individuals you know who are characterized by their integrity and honesty. Reflect on the sense of trust and respect they inspire. How can you cultivate these qualities more deeply in your own life?

Scripture Prompt:

Spend time meditating on **Proverbs 12:22**:

> *"Lying lips are an abomination to the Lord, but those who act faithfully are his delight."* (ESV)

What strong language is used here to describe lying? What contrast is drawn with those who act faithfully? How does this verse highlight God's perspective on honesty and integrity?

Now, also read **Ephesians 4:25**:

> *"Therefore, having put away falsehood, let each one of you speak the truth with his neighbor, for we are members one of another."* (ESV)

What clear command is given in this verse? What is the reasoning provided for speaking the truth? How does our interconnectedness as members of the body of Christ emphasize the importance of honesty?

Guided Reflection:

Write down your reflections on the questions above and your insights from Proverbs 12:22 and Ephesians 4:25. Consider specific areas of your life where you are challenged to be fully honest and to live with unwavering integrity.

Devotional: Living a Life of Truthfulness

Our words and actions have a significant impact on those around us and on our witness for Christ. When we live with integrity and speak truthfully, we build a foundation of trust in our relationships and demonstrate the trustworthiness of God. Conversely, dishonesty erodes trust and can damage our testimony.

This week let's be particularly mindful of our words and actions, striving for complete honesty in all our interactions. This includes not only avoiding outright lies but also being truthful in our motives, our promises, and our representations of ourselves. Living with integrity also means being consistent in our values, allowing our beliefs to shape our behavior in every area of life, both publicly and privately.

By committing to integrity and honesty, we honor God, strengthen our relationships, and live with a clear conscience. This way of living is a powerful reflection of the One who is truth itself (John 14:6).

Prayer Prompt:

Spend time in prayer asking God to reveal any areas in your life where you may be compromising on honesty or integrity. Pray for the courage to speak the truth, even when it's difficult, and for the strength to live in alignment with your beliefs in all circumstances.

Personal Reflection & Growth Journal

Significant Moments / Insights from This Week's Study

What happened? What was the insight?

_____

_____

_____

_____

_____

Emotional/Spiritual Responses:

_____

_____

_____

_____

Spiritual Insights/Lessons Learned:

- First thoughts:

_____

_____

_____

_____

- New perspectives gained:

_____

_____

_____

_____

- My Response/Action:

_____

_____

_____

_____

What helped me connect with God/grow this ?week?

_____

_____

_____

_____

What hindered my connection/?growth?

_____

_____

_____

_____

Week 21: Generosity and Giving

Generosity and giving are more than just financial acts; they reflect a heart that understands the abundance God has provided and a willingness to share those blessings with others. Scripture encourages us to give freely, cheerfully, and with a spirit of love (2 Corinthians 9:7), recognizing that all we have ultimately comes from God.

Think about times you have experienced the joy of giving or receiving a generous gift. Reflect on the impact of generosity, both on the giver and the receiver. How can you cultivate a more generous spirit in your own life?

Scripture Prompt:

Spend time meditating on **2 Corinthians 9:6-7**:

> *"The point is this: whoever sows sparingly will also reap sparingly, and whoever sows bountifully will also reap bountifully. Each one must give as he has decided in his heart, not reluctantly or under compulsion, for God loves a cheerful giver."* (ESV)

What principle of sowing and reaping is highlighted in this passage? What attitude should accompany our giving? What does it mean that "God loves a cheerful giver"?

Now, also read **Luke 6:38**:

> *"give, and it will be given to you. Good measure, pressed down, shaken together, running over, will be put into your lap. For with the measure you use it will be measured back to you.""* (ESV)

What promise is given to those who give? What kind of measure is described? How does this verse encourage a generous approach to sharing our resources?

Guided Reflection:

Write down your thoughts on the questions above and your insights from 2 Corinthians 9:6-7 and Luke 6:38. Consider the various ways you can be generous – with your time, talents, and resources – and identify practical ways to give this week.

Devotional: The Joy of Sharing God's Blessings

Generosity is not about what we give but about the heart with which we give. When we recognize that all we possess is a gift from God, we are freed to share it with open hands and joyful hearts. Giving is an act of worship and an expression of our gratitude for God's provision.

This week let's be intentional about looking for opportunities to be generous. This might involve contributing financially to causes you believe in, offering your time to help someone in need, sharing your skills or talents, or simply being generous with your kindness and encouragement.

Remember that generosity extends beyond material possessions. We can also be generous with our forgiveness, our patience, our time, and our love. As we cultivate a generous spirit, we not only bless others but also experience the deep joy that comes from reflecting God's own giving nature.

Prayer Prompt:

Spend time in prayer asking God to cultivate a generous heart within you. Pray for wisdom to discern how you can best use your resources – time, talents, and finances – to bless others and honor Him. Ask for a cheerful spirit in your giving.

Personal Reflection & Growth Journal

Significant Moments / Insights from This Week's Study

What happened? What was the insight?

_____

_____

_____

_____

_____

Emotional/Spiritual Responses:

_____

_____

_____

_____

Spiritual Insights/Lessons Learned:

- First thoughts:

_____

_____

_____

- New perspectives gained:

_____

_____

_____

- My Response/Action:

_____

_____

_____

_____

What helped me connect with God/grow this ?week?

_____

_____

_____

_____

What hindered my connection/?growth?

_____

_____

_____

_____

Week 22: Prayer and Communication with God

Prayer is the lifeline of our relationship with God. It is our direct line of communication, a sacred space where we can speak to our Heavenly Father, share our hearts, seek His guidance, and express our gratitude. It's not about reciting perfect words but about authentic connection with the One who loves us unconditionally.

Think about your current prayer life. What does it look like? What are the joys and challenges you experience in communicating with God? How can you cultivate a deeper and more consistent practice of prayer?

Scripture Prompt:

Spend time meditating on **Philippians 4:6-7**:

> *"Do not be anxious about anything, but in everything by prayer and supplication with thanksgiving let your requests be made known to God. And the peace of God, which surpasses all understanding, will guard your hearts and your minds in Christ Jesus."* (ESV)

What are we encouraged to do instead of being anxious? What elements should be part of our prayer life according to this passage? What is the promised result of bringing our requests to God with thanksgiving?

Now, also read **1 Thessalonians 5:17**:

> *"pray without ceasing."* (ESV)

What does it mean to "pray without ceasing"? Is this a call to be constantly vocal? How can we cultivate a lifestyle of continuous communication with God throughout our day?

Guided Reflection:

Write down your reflections on the questions above and your insights from Philippians 4:6-7 and 1 Thessalonians 5:17. Consider practical ways you can deepen your prayer life this week, perhaps by setting aside specific times, trying new forms of prayer, or being more mindful of God's presence throughout your day.

Devotional: Cultivating a Conversation with the Divine

Prayer is a multifaceted conversation with God. It includes adoration for who He is, confession of our sins, thanksgiving for His blessings, and supplication for our needs and the needs of others. It's a time to listen for His still, small voice and to align our hearts with His will.

This week let's be intentional about cultivating a richer prayer life. This might involve setting aside dedicated time each day for focused prayer, keeping a prayer journal, praying Scripture back to God, or simply having ongoing conversations with Him as you go about your day.

Remember that God longs to hear from you. He is not distant or uninterested but is intimately involved in your life. By making prayer a consistent priority, we open ourselves to His guidance, comfort, and peace that surpasses all understanding.

Prayer Prompt:

Spend time in prayer asking God to deepen your desire for communication with Him. Pray for discipline and consistency in your prayer life. Ask for guidance in how to pray more effectively and for a greater awareness of His presence as you pray.

Personal Reflection & Growth Journal

Significant Moments / Insights from This Week's Study

What happened? What was the insight?

_____

_____

_____

_____

Emotional/Spiritual Responses:

_____

_____

_____

_____

Spiritual Insights/Lessons Learned:

- First thoughts:

_____

_____

_____

- New perspectives gained:

_____

_____

_____

- My Response/Action:

_____
_____
_____
_____

What helped me connect with God/grow this ?week?

_____
_____
_____
_____

What hindered my connection/?growth?

_____
_____
_____
_____

Week 23: Wisdom in Decision Making

Life is a series of choices, both big and small. As we seek to live out our faith, it's crucial to approach these decisions with wisdom – the ability to discern what is right and good, and to make choices that align with God's will and His principles. God promises to give wisdom to those who ask (James 1:5), and Scripture provides guidance for navigating the complexities of life.

Think about significant decisions you've faced. How did you seek wisdom? What were the outcomes? Reflect on the importance of making choices that honor God and lead to good outcomes.

Scripture Prompt:

Spend time meditating on **James 1:5**:

> *"If any of you lacks wisdom, let him ask God, who gives generously to all without reproach, and it will be given him."* (ESV)

What encouragement and promise does this verse offer regarding wisdom? What is the condition for receiving wisdom from God? What does it mean that God gives "generously" and "without reproach"?

Now, also read **Proverbs 4:7**:

> *"The beginning of wisdom is this: Get wisdom, and whatever you get, get insight."* (ESV)

What does this proverb identify as the "beginning of wisdom"? What does it emphasize about the importance of actively seeking not just knowledge but also understanding (insight)?

Guided Reflection:

Write down your answers for the questions above and your insights from James 1:5 and Proverbs 4:7. Consider any current decisions you are facing and how you can intentionally seek God's wisdom in making them.

Devotional: Seeking God's Guidance in Our Choices

Making wise decisions involves more than just logic and reasoning; it requires seeking God's perspective through prayer, studying His Word, and listening to the counsel of godly individuals. It's about aligning our desires with His will and choosing paths that lead to righteousness and blessing.

This week let's be intentional about seeking God's wisdom in the decisions we face, both large and small. Before making a choice, take time to pray and ask for His guidance. Consider what Scripture says about the matter or related principles. Seek advice from trusted Christian mentors or friends.

Remember that God's wisdom often transcends our immediate understanding. Trusting in Him means being willing to follow His leading, even when it doesn't always make sense to us in the moment. By consistently seeking His wisdom, we can navigate life's complexities with greater clarity and confidence.

Prayer Prompt:

Spend time in prayer asking God for wisdom and discernment in the decisions you are currently facing. Pray for clarity of mind, a heart that is open to His will, and the courage to follow His leading, even when it's challenging.

Personal Reflection & Growth Journal

Significant Moments / Insights from This Week's Study

What happened? What was the insight?

_____

_____

_____

_____

_____

Emotional/Spiritual Responses:

_____

_____

_____

_____

_____

Spiritual Insights/Lessons Learned:

- First thoughts:

_____

_____

_____

- New perspectives gained:

_____

_____

_____

_____

- My Response/Action:

_____

_____

_____

_____

What helped me connect with God/grow this ?week?

_____

_____

_____

_____

What hindered my connection/?growth?

_____

_____

_____

_____

Week 24: Managing Our Thoughts and Emotions

Our thoughts and emotions have a powerful influence on our actions and our overall well-being. As we seek to live out our faith, it's essential to learn how to manage them in a way that honors God and reflects His peace. This doesn't mean suppressing our feelings, but rather understanding them, processing them healthily, and aligning them with biblical truth.

Think about the times your thoughts or emotions have led you astray or caused you distress. Reflect on the importance of bringing them under the Lordship of Christ and cultivating a mind and heart that are at peace.

Scripture Prompt:

Spend time meditating on **Philippians 4:8**:

> *"Finally, brothers, whatever is true, whatever is honorable, whatever is just, whatever is pure, whatever is lovely, whatever is commendable, if there is any excellence, if there is anything worthy of praise, think about these things."* (ESV)

What specific categories of thoughts are we encouraged to focus on? How does intentionally directing our thoughts in this way impact our emotions and our overall perspective?

Now, also read **Proverbs 4:23**:

> *"Keep your heart with all vigilance, for from it flows the springs of life."* (ESV)

In this context, "heart" often refers to the inner person, including thoughts and emotions. What strong instruction is given regarding the keeping of our hearts? Why is this so important according to this verse?

Guided Reflection:

Think about the answers you would give for the questions above and your insights from Philippians 4:8 and Proverbs 4:23. Consider specific patterns of negative thinking or challenging emotions you experience. What practical steps can you take this week to intentionally direct your thoughts and guard your heart?

Devotional: Cultivating a Mind of Peace and Truth

Managing our thoughts and emotions is an ongoing process that requires intentionality and reliance on the Holy Spirit. It involves recognizing when our thoughts are not aligned with truth, challenging negative or unhelpful thought patterns, and choosing to focus on what is good, pure, and praiseworthy.

This week let's be more aware of the thoughts that occupy our minds and the emotions that stir within us. When negative thoughts arise, consciously replace them with biblical truths and affirmations. When strong emotions surface, take time to process them in a healthy way, perhaps through prayer, journaling, or talking with a trusted friend.

Remember that we have the mind of Christ (1 Corinthians 2:16) and the power of the Holy Spirit to help us in this area. By intentionally choosing to dwell on what is true and good, and by entrusting our emotions to God, we can cultivate a greater sense of inner peace and live in a way that honors Him.

Prayer Prompt:

Spend time in prayer asking God to give you greater awareness of your thought patterns and emotional responses. Pray for His help in challenging negative thoughts and replacing them with His truth. Ask for His peace to guard your heart and mind in Christ Jesus.

Personal Reflection & Growth Journal

Significant Moments / Insights from This Week's Study

What happened? What was the insight?

_____

_____

_____

_____

_____

Emotional/Spiritual Responses:

_____

_____

_____

_____

_____

Spiritual Insights/Lessons Learned:

- First thoughts:

_____

_____

_____

- New perspectives gained:

_____

_____

_____

- My Response/Action:

_____

_____

_____

_____

What helped me connect with God/grow this ?week?

_____

_____

_____

_____

What hindered my connection/?growth?

_____

_____

_____

_____

Week 25: Our Words and Their Impact

Our words hold immense power: the power to build up or tear down, to encourage or discourage, to speak truth or to deceive. As followers of Christ, our speech should reflect His love, grace, and truth. We are called to be mindful of the impact our words have on those around us and to use them in ways that honor God and bless others.

Think about times when someone's words deeply impacted you, for good or for ill. Reflect on the responsibility we have to use our words thoughtfully and intentionally.

Scripture Prompt:

Spend time meditating on **James 3:5-10**:

> *"So also the tongue is a small member, yet it boasts of great things. How great a forest is set ablaze by a small fire! And the tongue is a fire, a world of unrighteousness set among our members, staining the whole body, setting on fire the entire course of life, and set on fire by hell. For every kind of beast and bird, of reptile and sea creature, can be tamed and has been tamed by mankind, but no human being can tame the tongue. It is a restless evil, full of deadly poison. With it we bless our Lord and Father, and with it we curse human beings who are made in the likeness of God. From the same mouth come blessing and cursing. My brothers, these things ought not to be so."*(ESV)

What powerful and sobering imagery does James use to describe the tongue? What does this passage reveal about the potential for both good and harm in our words? What is the inconsistency James highlights in how we often use our tongues?

Now, also read **Proverbs 15:1**:

> *"A soft answer turns away wrath, but a harsh word stirs up anger."*(ESV)

What practical wisdom does this proverb offer regarding our communication, particularly in conflict? How can choosing our words carefully influence the outcome of a conversation?

Guided Reflection:

Write down your answers for the questions above and your insights from James 3:5-10 and Proverbs 15:1. Consider your own patterns of speech. Are there areas where you need to be more mindful of the impact of your words? What practical steps can you take this week to speak with more grace and truth?

Devotional: Speaking Life and Truth

Our words are a reflection of what is in our hearts (Matthew 12:34). As we grow in our relationship with God, our speech should increasingly reflect His character. This means speaking with kindness, encouragement, and truth. It involves choosing words that build up rather than tear down, that offer hope rather than despair, and that honor God in all circumstances.

This week let's be intentional about the words we speak. Before we speak, let us consider their potential impact. Are they true? Are they kind? Are they necessary? Let us strive to be those who speak life and truth into the lives of others, using our words as instruments of God's love and grace.

Remember that even seemingly small words can have a lasting effect. Let us choose to use them wisely, reflecting the heart of the One who is the Word of life.

Prayer Prompt:

Spend time in prayer asking God to help you be more mindful of the words you speak. Pray for a filter on your tongue, that your words would be seasoned with grace and truth. Ask for wisdom in knowing when to speak and when to remain silent, and for the power to use your words to bless and encourage others.

Personal Reflection & Growth Journal

Significant Moments / Insights from This Week's Study

What happened? What was the insight?

_____

_____

_____

_____

_____

Emotional/Spiritual Responses:

_____

_____

_____

_____

_____

Spiritual Insights/Lessons Learned:

- First thoughts:

_____

_____

_____

_____

- New perspectives gained:

_____

_____

_____

_____

- My Response/Action:

_____

_____

_____

_____

What helped me connect with God/grow this ?week?

_____

_____

_____

_____

What hindered my connection/?growth?

_____

_____

_____

_____

Week 26: Rest and Sabbath

In our busy, productivity-driven culture, the concept of rest can often feel like a luxury rather than a necessity. However, God Himself modeled rest after creation (Genesis 2:2-3) and commanded a Sabbath for His people. Observing a rhythm of rest is not just about physical rejuvenation; it's an act of trust in God's provision and a recognition that our worth is not solely tied to our accomplishments.

Think about your own patterns of rest. Do you intentionally set aside time to cease from your regular work and activities? What are the challenges you face in prioritizing rest? Reflect on the potential spiritual and physical benefits of embracing a Sabbath rhythm.

Scripture Prompt:

Spend time meditating on **Mark 2:27**:

"And he said to them, "The Sabbath was made for man, not man for the Sabbath."" (ESV)

What does Jesus mean by this statement? How does it shift the focus of the Sabbath? What is the intended purpose of rest according to Jesus?

Now, also read **Hebrews 4:9-10**:

"So then, there remains a Sabbath rest for the people of God, for whoever has entered God's rest has also rested from his works as God did from his." (ESV)

What kind of "Sabbath rest" remains for God's people? How does entering God's rest relate to ceasing from our own works? What does this imply about our ultimate rest in Christ?

Guided Reflection:

Consider your answers for the questions above and your insights from Mark 2:27 and Hebrews 4:9-10. Consider how you can intentionally incorporate more rest and perhaps a Sabbath practice into your week. What might need to shift in your schedule or mindset to prioritize this?

Devotional: Finding Renewal in Ceasing

Rest, especially a dedicated Sabbath, is an opportunity to step back from the demands of our work and responsibilities and to intentionally focus on God and the things that truly nourish our souls. It's a time for physical refreshment, spiritual renewal, and relational connection.

This week, consider how you can intentionally create space for rest. This might involve setting aside a specific day or portion of a day to cease from your usual work, to spend time in prayer and reflection, to enjoy peaceful activities, and to connect with loved ones.

Remember that rest is not laziness; it is an act of obedience and a recognition of our human limits and God's unlimited provision. By embracing a rhythm of rest, we honor God, care for ourselves, and return to our responsibilities with renewed energy and perspective.

Prayer Prompt:

Spend time in prayer asking God to reveal any areas where you are neglecting rest. Pray for wisdom to prioritize rest in a way that honors Him and nourishes your soul. Ask for guidance in establishing healthy rhythms of work and rest in your life.

Personal Reflection & Growth Journal

Significant Moments / Insights from This Week's Study

What happened? What was the insight?

_____

_____

_____

_____

_____

Emotional/Spiritual Responses:

_____

_____

_____

_____

Spiritual Insights/Lessons Learned:

- First thoughts:

_____

_____

_____

- New perspectives gained:

_____

_____

_____

- My Response/Action:

_____

_____

_____

What helped me connect with God/grow this ?week?

_____

_____

_____

_____

_____

What hindered my connection/?growth?

_____

_____

_____

_____

Week 27: Sharing Our Faith

As those who have experienced the love and truth of God, we are called to share this good news with others. Sharing our faith isn't about forceful proselytizing but about authentically communicating the hope we have in Christ through our words and actions. It's about allowing our lives to be a testimony to God's grace and being ready to articulate the reasons for our belief when opportunities arise.

Think about the moment you came to faith or a time when your faith became particularly meaningful to you. Reflect on the desire to share that with others and the ways you have (or haven't yet) done so.

Scripture Prompt:

Spend time meditating on **Matthew 28:19-20**:

"Go therefore and make disciples of all nations, baptizing them in the name of the Father and of the Son and of the Holy Spirit, teaching them to observe all that I have commanded you. And behold, I am with you always, to the end of the age." (ESV)

What is the Great Commission that Jesus gives His followers? What are the key components of making disciples? What promise does Jesus give alongside this command?

Now, also read **1 Peter 3:15**:

"but in your hearts honor Christ the Lord as holy, always being prepared to make a defense to anyone who asks you for a reason for the hope that is in you; yet do it with gentleness and respect." (ESV)

What does it mean to "honor Christ the Lord as holy" in our hearts? What posture should we have in sharing our faith? What attitude should accompany our defense of the hope we have?

Guided Reflection:

Write down your reflections on the questions above and your insights from Matthew 28:19-20 and 1 Peter 3:15. Consider the people in your life who may not yet know Christ. What are some ways you can authentically share your faith with them through your words and actions this week?

Devotional: Letting Our Light Shine

Sharing our faith is not about having all the answers or being a perfect theologian. It's about allowing the light of Christ within us to shine outwardly. Our transformed lives, our acts of love and kindness, and our willingness to speak about the hope we have can all be powerful witnesses to God's grace.

This week let's be prayerfully open to opportunities to share our faith. This might involve sharing a personal testimony, explaining why you follow Christ, inviting someone to church, or simply living in such a way that others see the difference Christ makes in your life.

Remember that God doesn't call us to convert people but to faithfully share the truth in love. Trust the Holy Spirit to work in hearts, and be ready to speak with gentleness and respect when the opportunity arises.

Prayer Prompt:

Spend time in prayer asking God for boldness and wisdom in sharing your faith. Pray for opportunities to speak about His love and truth, and for the right words to say. Ask for a heart that desires others to know the joy and peace you have found in Christ.

Personal Reflection & Growth Journal

Significant Moments / Insights from This Week's Study

What happened? What was the insight?

_____

_____

_____

_____

_____

Emotional/Spiritual Responses:

_____

_____

_____

_____

_____

Spiritual Insights/Lessons Learned:

- First thoughts:

_____

_____

_____

_____

- New perspectives gained:

_____

_____

_____

_____

- My Response/Action:

_____

_____

_____

_____

What helped me connect with God/grow this ?week?

_____

_____

_____

_____

What hindered my connection/?growth?

_____

_____

_____

_____

Week 28: Review and Reflection on Living Out Faith

Over the past twelve weeks, we've focused on the practical ways our faith in God should shape our daily lives. We've explored themes such as love, forgiveness, patience, humility, honesty, generosity, prayer, wisdom, managing our thoughts, our words, rest, and sharing our faith. This week is an opportunity to look back, reflect on what we've learned, and consider how we are growing in embodying these principles.

Think about the various areas of your life we've touched upon. In which of these areas have you felt challenged? Where have you seen growth? What resonates most with you as essential for living out your faith authentically?

Scripture Prompt:

Spend time meditating on **Galatians 2:20**:

"I have been crucified with Christ. It is no longer I who live, but Christ who lives in me. And the life I now live in the flesh I live by faith in the Son of God, who loved me and gave himself for me." (ESV)

How does this verse encapsulate the essence of living out our faith? What does it mean for Christ to live in us? How does this truth connect with the practical themes we've explored this quarter?

Guided Reflection:

Think about the themes of "Living Out Our Faith" explored in Weeks 16 through 27. Consider the following questions:

- Which of the practical applications of faith we studied this quarter felt most relevant to your current season of life? Why?

- In what area of living out your faith do you sense the most significant growth over the past few weeks? What contributed to that growth?

- What is one area where you feel God is still calling you to more intentional action in living out your faith? What might be a first step in that direction?

- How has reflecting on these practical aspects deepened your understanding of what it means to follow Christ in your everyday life?

Devotional: Continuing to Embody Our Beliefs

Living out our faith is not a destination but a continuous journey of growth and refinement. The principles we've explored this quarter are not meant to be mastered in a few weeks but rather to become ongoing practices that shape our character and our interactions with the world.

As we move towards the next quarter, let us carry with us the lessons learned about loving, forgiving, persevering, serving, being honest, giving generously, praying consistently, seeking wisdom, managing our inner lives, using our words wisely, prioritizing rest, and sharing our hope.

May we continue to be intentional in allowing our beliefs to translate into tangible actions, reflecting the love and light of Christ in all we do.

Prayer Prompt:

Spend time in prayer asking God to help you integrate the principles of living out your faith into your daily life. Pray for continued growth in these areas and for a heart that is eager to embody His love and truth in all your actions and interactions.

Personal Reflection & Growth Journal

Significant Moments / Insights from This Week's Study

What happened? What was the insight?

_____

_____

_____

_____

Emotional/Spiritual Responses:

_____

_____

_____

_____

Spiritual Insights/Lessons Learned:

- First thoughts:

_____

_____

_____

- New perspectives gained:

_____

_____

_____

_____

- My Response/Action:

_____

_____

_____

_____

What helped me connect with God/grow this ?week?

_____

_____

_____

_____

What hindered my connection/?growth?

_____

_____

_____

_____

III. Quarter 3: Connecting with Others (Weeks 29-41) - Theme: Our Relationships and Community

Week 29: Our Relationships and Community

Having spent the last quarter focusing on how our individual faith impacts our actions and choices, we now turn our attention to the relational aspect of our faith journey. Quarter 3 will explore the theme of "Connecting with Others." As believers, we are part of a larger body, the Church, and our relationships with one another are vital for support, encouragement, and reflecting the love of Christ to the world.

Think about the significance of community in your faith. How have others influenced your walk with God? How do you see your role in the lives of fellow believers and those around you?

Scripture Prompt:

Spend time meditating on **1 John 4:7**:

"Beloved, let us love one another, for love is from God, and whoever loves has been born of God and knows God." (ESV)

What is the clear command given in this verse regarding our relationships with one another? What is the connection made between love and our relationship with God? How does this emphasize the importance of love within the Christian community?

Guided Reflection:

Think about the theme of "Connecting with Others." Consider the following questions:

- What does "Christian community" mean to you? What are some of the benefits and challenges of being part of a faith community?

- How do you currently connect with other believers for encouragement and support? Are there ways you would like to deepen these connections?

- As you look ahead to exploring our relationships and community in Quarter 3, what are your hopes for growth in this area?

Devotional: The Importance of Godly Connections

God designed us for relationships, both with Him and with one another. Within the community of believers, we find encouragement, accountability, support in times of need, and the opportunity to serve and be served. Our interactions with fellow Christians and even those outside our immediate faith community are meant to reflect the love and unity that characterize the body of Christ.

As we begin this quarter, let us open our hearts to the importance of building and nurturing godly connections. We will explore themes such as the value of community, healthy friendships, navigating family relationships, extending grace, resolving conflict, and the impact of our witness on those around us.

May this quarter be a time of growth in our ability to love and connect with others in ways that honor God and strengthen the fabric of His Kingdom.

Prayer Prompt:

Spend time in prayer asking God to highlight the importance of your relationships within the body of Christ and beyond. Pray for wisdom and guidance in building healthy and meaningful connections with others. Ask for a heart that is open to loving and serving those around you.

Personal Reflection & Growth Journal

Significant Moments / Insights from This Week's Study

What happened? What was the insight?

_____

_____

_____

_____

Emotional/Spiritual Responses:

_____

_____

_____

_____

Spiritual Insights/Lessons Learned:

- First thoughts:

_____

_____

_____

- New perspectives gained:

_____

_____

_____

- My Response/Action:

_____

_____

_____

_____

What helped me connect with God/grow this ?week?

_____

_____

_____

_____

What hindered my connection/?growth?

_____

_____

_____

_____

Week 30: The Importance of Christian Community

After introducing the theme of connecting with others, we begin by focusing on the Christian community itself. The Bible often describes believers as a body with many parts (1 Corinthians 12:12-27), a family (Ephesians 2:19), and living stones building a spiritual house (1 Peter 2:5). We are not meant to navigate our faith journey in isolation but in supportive fellowship with other believers.

Think about your current experiences with Christian community. What are the benefits you've personally found in being connected with other believers? What challenges or obstacles have you encountered in seeking or maintaining community?

Scripture Prompt:

Spend time meditating on **Hebrews 10:24-25**:

> *"And let us consider how to stir up one another to love and good works, not neglecting to meet together, as is the habit of some, but encouraging one another, and all the more as you see the Day drawing near."* (ESV)

What is the purpose of meeting together as believers according to this passage? What does it mean to "stir up one another to love and good works"? How does the approaching "Day" (referring to Christ's return) emphasize the urgency of Christian fellowship?

Now, also read **Acts 2:42-47** (focus on verses 42 and 46-47):

> *"And they devoted themselves to the apostles' teaching and the fellowship, to the breaking of bread and the prayers... And day by day, attending the temple together and breaking bread in their homes, they received their food with glad and generous hearts, praising God and having favor with all the people. And the Lord added to their number day by day those who were being saved."* (ESV)

What were the early believers devoted to? What characteristics describe their fellowship and shared life? What was the outcome of their strong community and devotion?

Guided Reflection:

Write down your reflections on the questions above and your insights from Hebrews 10:24-25 and Acts 2:42-47. Consider your involvement in Christian community. What is one practical step you can take this week to more fully engage with or contribute to a healthy Christian community?

Devotional: Finding Strength and Support in the Body

Christian community is a vital gift from God. It's where we are challenged, encouraged, comforted, and sharpened. Within this fellowship, we can share our burdens, celebrate our victories, grow through accountability, and learn from the diverse perspectives and gifts of others. It is where we find a sense of belonging and truly experience being part of God's family.

This week let's intentionally consider the importance of Christian community in our lives. If you are already actively involved, give thanks for those relationships and look for ways to deepen them. If you are not yet connected, prayerfully consider seeking out a church or small group where you can find genuine fellowship and support.

Remember, we are not designed to live out our faith alone. Just as individual threads woven together create a strong tapestry, believers united in Christ form a powerful testimony to God's love and work in the world.

Prayer Prompt:

Spend time in prayer thanking God for the gift of Christian community. Pray for your local church or Christian fellowship, asking God to strengthen it and to use it for His glory. If you are seeking community, pray for His guidance in finding the right place of belonging and growth.

Personal Reflection & Growth Journal

Significant Moments / Insights from This Week's Study

What happened? What was the insight?

_____

_____

_____

_____

_____

Emotional/Spiritual Responses:

_____

_____

_____

_____

_____

Spiritual Insights/Lessons Learned:

- First thoughts:

_____

_____

_____

_____

- New perspectives gained:

_____

_____

_____

_____

- My Response/Action:

_____

_____

_____

_____

What helped me connect with God/grow this ?week?

_____

_____

_____

_____

What hindered my connection/?growth?

_____

_____

_____

_____

Week 31: Building Healthy Friendships

Healthy friendships add richness and depth to our lives, providing support, encouragement, and shared experiences along our faith journey. They offer a space for vulnerability, accountability, and mutual growth.

Think about the friends who have had a positive impact on your life. What qualities do they possess that make those friendships meaningful? How do healthy friendships contribute to your spiritual growth and overall well-being?

Scripture Prompt:

Spend time meditating on **Proverbs 17:17**:

> *"A friend loves at all times, and a brother is born for adversity."* (ESV)

What does it mean for a friend to love "at all times"? How does this contrast with fair-weather acquaintances? How does the second part of this proverb broaden our understanding of the depth and purpose of true friendship?

Now, also read **1 Thessalonians 5:11**:

> *"Therefore encourage one another and build one another up, just as you are doing."* (ESV)

What is the primary action we are called to in our interactions with one another? How do encouragement and building up contribute to healthy friendships within the community of believers?

Guided Reflection:

Write down your reflections on the questions above and your insights from Proverbs 17:17 and 1 Thessalonians 5:11. Consider the friendships in your life. Are they characterized by consistent love and mutual encouragement? What steps can you take to nurture existing friendships or build new, healthy connections within your community?

Devotional: Cultivating Meaningful Connections

Healthy friendships are a precious gift. They provide a safe space for vulnerability, honest feedback, shared laughter, and mutual support through life's challenges and triumphs. Building these kinds of connections requires intentionality, time, and a willingness to be both a giver and a receiver in the relationship.

This week, consider reaching out to a friend you appreciate. Perhaps schedule time to connect over a meal, take a walk together, or simply send a message of encouragement. Be mindful of being a good listener and offering support in practical ways.

Remember that friendships, like any valuable thing, need tending to flourish. Invest time and effort in nurturing the relationships God has placed in your life, and be open to the possibility of new, meaningful connections with those around you.

Prayer Prompt:

Spend time in prayer thanking God for the gift of friendship. Pray for your current friends, asking for strength and blessing in their lives. Ask for wisdom in nurturing these relationships and for guidance in building new, healthy friendships with those around you.

Personal Reflection & Growth Journal

Significant Moments / Insights from This Week's Study

What happened? What was the insight?

_____

_____

_____

_____

_____

Emotional/Spiritual Responses:

_____

_____

_____

_____

Spiritual Insights/Lessons Learned:

- First thoughts:

_____

_____

_____

- New perspectives gained:

_____

_____

_____

- My Response/Action:

_____

_____

_____

_____

What helped me connect with God/grow this ?week?

_____

_____

_____

_____

What hindered my connection/?growth?

_____

_____

_____

_____

Week 32: Navigating Family Relationships

Family relationships, whether by blood or by choice, are some of the most significant and often the most complex connections in our lives. They can be sources of immense joy and support, but also of deep-seated challenges and unique dynamics. Living out our faith in the context of family requires grace, understanding, patience, and a willingness to extend unconditional love.

Think about the various family relationships in your life. What are the unique blessings they offer? What are some of the particular challenges you encounter in these relationships, and how do you typically navigate them?

Scripture Prompt:

Spend time meditating on **Ephesians 4:2-3**:

> *"with all humility and gentleness, with patience, bearing with one another in love, eager to maintain the unity of the Spirit in the bond of peace."* (ESV)

What specific virtues are we called to practice in our relationships? How do "bearing with one another in love" and "eager to maintain the unity of the Spirit" apply particularly to the, often intense, dynamics of family?

Now, also read **Colossians 3:12-14**:

> *"Put on then, as God's chosen ones, holy and beloved, compassionate hearts, kindness, humility, meekness, and patience, bearing with one another and, if one has a complaint against another, forgiving each other; as the Lord has forgiven you, so you also must forgive. And above all these put on love, which binds everything together in perfect harmony."* (ESV)

Many of these attributes overlap with ones we've already discussed. Why are they so crucial for healthy family interactions? How does "love, which binds everything together in perfect harmony," serve as the ultimate goal for our family relationships?

Guided Reflection:

Think about the questions above and your insights from Ephesians 4:2-3 and Colossians 3:12-14. Identify a couple family relationships where you want to apply these biblical principles more intentionally this week. What specific actions or changes in attitude can you focus on?

Devotional: Grace at Home

Our homes and families are often the truest testing grounds of our faith. It's easy to extend kindness and patience to strangers, but it can be much harder to do so with those who know us best, and whose imperfections, like our own, are most visible. Yet, it is precisely in these intimate relationships that our faith can shine most brightly and bring about the most profound impact.

This week let's commit to bringing "grace at home." This means actively choosing to listen, to respond with gentleness rather than reactivity, to offer forgiveness freely, and to seek understanding. It means recognizing that every member of your family is a person created in God's image, worthy of respect and love, regardless of past hurts or current challenges.

Remember that God is the author of family, and He desires for these relationships to flourish. By intentionally seeking to embody His love, patience, and forgiveness within our family dynamics, we contribute to an atmosphere of peace and mutual growth.

Prayer Prompt:

Spend time in prayer for your family relationships. Ask God for wisdom, patience, and love to navigate them well. Pray for healing in any strained relationships and for strength to extend grace and forgiveness as Christ has extended it to you.

Personal Reflection & Growth Journal

Significant Moments / Insights from This Week's Study

What happened? What was the insight?

_____

_____

_____

_____

_____

Emotional/Spiritual Responses:

_____

_____

_____

_____

Spiritual Insights/Lessons Learned:
- First thoughts:

_____

_____

_____

- New perspectives gained:

_____

_____

_____

_____

- My Response/Action:

_____

_____

_____

_____

What helped me connect with God/grow this ?week?

_____

_____

_____

_____

What hindered my connection/?growth?

_____

_____

_____

_____

_____

_____

_____

Week 33: Extending Grace to Others

We've explored God's abundant grace towards us, and now we turn to the vital practice of extending that same grace to the people around us. Grace is unmerited favor, a gift given freely, not because it's earned but because of a generous heart. In our interactions, extending grace means offering understanding, patience, and forgiveness, even when it's not deserved, reflecting God's own heart towards us.

Think about a time someone showed you unexpected grace when you made a mistake or fell short. How did that act of grace make you feel? Consider the opportunities you have in your daily life to offer grace to those you encounter.

Scripture Prompt:

Spend time meditating on **Ephesians 4:32**:

> *"Be kind to one another, tenderhearted, forgiving one another, as God in Christ forgave you."* (ESV)

What specific actions are we called to practice in our relationships? What is the ultimate motivation or standard for our forgiveness of others? How does understanding God's forgiveness of you empower you to extend it to others?

Now, also read **Romans 15:7**:

> *"Therefore welcome one another as Christ has welcomed you, for the glory of God."* (ESV)

What does it mean to "welcome one another as Christ has welcomed you"? How does extending such welcome contribute to the glory of God? How can this verse guide your interactions with new acquaintances or those who might be different from you in our diverse city?

Guided Reflection:

Think about the questions above and your insights from Ephesians 4:32 and Romans 15:7. Identify one specific person or situation this week where you can intentionally choose to extend grace, perhaps by overlooking a minor irritation, offering understanding instead of judgment, or showing unexpected kindness.

Devotional: The Ripple Effect of Unmerited Favor

Extending grace is not always easy. Our natural inclination can be to react with judgment, frustration, or a desire for fairness. However, when we choose grace, we step into the divine, mirroring the boundless mercy God has shown us. This act transforms not only the recipient but also our own hearts, freeing us from bitterness and allowing God's peace to flow through us.

This week let's look for opportunities to be agents of grace in our interactions. This might involve being patient with a difficult colleague, offering a second chance to someone who disappointed you, giving someone the benefit of the doubt, or simply responding with calm when faced with rudeness. It's about remembering that everyone you meet is a complex individual, often facing unseen struggles, and is worthy of compassion.

Remember, the grace we extend is a powerful testimony to the grace we have received from God. Let it be a beautiful overflow of His unmerited favor in your life, creating a ripple effect of kindness and understanding in your community and beyond.

Prayer Prompt:

Spend time in prayer asking God to fill you with a spirit of grace and compassion. Pray for opportunities to extend unmerited favor to those around you, and for a heart that is quick to forgive and slow to judge, just as He is with you.

Personal Reflection & Growth Journal

Significant Moments / Insights from This Week's Study

What happened? What was the insight?

_____

_____

_____

_____

_____

Emotional/Spiritual Responses:

_____

_____

_____

_____

Spiritual Insights/Lessons Learned:
- First thoughts:

_____

_____

_____

_____

- New perspectives gained:

_____

_____

_____

_____

- My Response/Action:

_____

_____

_____

_____

What helped me connect with God/grow this ?week?

_____

_____

_____

_____

What hindered my connection/?growth?

_____

_____

_____

_____

Week 34: Resolving Conflict Biblically

Even in the most loving communities, misunderstandings and disagreements are inevitable. Conflict, when handled poorly, can lead to deep hurt and broken relationships. However, when approached biblically, conflict can become an opportunity for growth, deeper understanding, and stronger bonds. God's Word provides clear guidance on how to navigate disagreements in a way that honors Him and fosters reconciliation.

Think about a recent conflict or disagreement you experienced. How did you react? What was the outcome? Reflect on how often personal or community peace is impacted by how conflict is handled, from the smallest daily interactions to larger community issues.

Scripture Prompt:

Spend time meditating on **Matthew 18:15**:

"If your brother sins against you, go and tell him his fault, between you and him alone. If he listens to you, you have gained your brother." (ESV)

What is the first step Jesus instructs us to take when a conflict arises? Why is it emphasized that this should be done "between you and him alone"? What is the positive outcome if this step is successful?

Now, also read **Ephesians 4:26-27**:

"Be angry and do not sin; do not let the sun go down on your anger, and give no opportunity to the devil." (ESV)

What important distinction is made regarding anger? What practical instruction is given about addressing anger? How does unresolved anger create an "opportunity for the devil" in our relationships?

Guided Reflection:

Write down your answers for the questions above and consider your insights from Matthew 18:15 and Ephesians 4:26-27. Think about a specific ongoing or past conflict in your life. What biblical principles from these verses can you apply to that situation? What is one step you can take toward biblical conflict resolution this week?

Devotional: Pursuing Peace and Understanding

Biblical conflict resolution is rooted in humility, a desire for reconciliation, and a commitment to truth spoken in love. It requires us to address issues directly and privately when possible, to listen empathetically, to confess our own part in the conflict, and to be quick to forgive as God has forgiven us. It is a proactive approach to maintaining peace and preserving relationships.

This week let's commit to addressing conflicts in a way that honors God. When tensions arise, pause and pray for wisdom and self-control. Seek to understand the other person's perspective before defending your own. Choose to speak truthfully, but always with kindness and respect. Remember that the goal is not to win an argument, but to restore a relationship and bring glory to God.

By engaging in biblical conflict resolution, we contribute to healthier relationships in our families, churches, workplaces, and broader communities. We become agents of peace, reflecting Christ in our interactions, even in the midst of disagreement.

Prayer Prompt:

Spend time in prayer for any specific conflicts you are currently navigating. Ask God for humility, courage, and wisdom to address these situations biblically. Pray for a spirit of reconciliation and for His peace to prevail in your relationships.

Personal Reflection & Growth Journal

Significant Moments / Insights from This Week's Study

What happened? What was the insight?

_____

_____

_____

_____

_____

Emotional/Spiritual Responses:

_____

_____

_____

_____

_____

Spiritual Insights/Lessons Learned:

- First thoughts:

_____

_____

_____

_____

- New perspectives gained:

_____

_____

_____

_____

- My Response/Action:

_____

_____

_____

_____

What helped me connect with God/grow this ?week?

_____

_____

_____

_____

What hindered my connection/?growth?

_____

_____

_____

_____

Week 35: Hospitality and Welcoming Others

True Christian connection often extends beyond our immediate circles to embrace those who are new, different, or in need of a place to belong. Hospitality is more than just offering a meal; it's a spirit of warmth, openness, and genuine welcome that reflects God's own heart towards us. It's about creating space in our lives and homes for others, fostering a sense of belonging and community.

Think about a time you felt truly welcomed and included. What made that experience special? Conversely, recall a time you felt excluded. How did that impact you? Reflect on how you currently practice hospitality in your daily life.

Scripture Prompt:

Spend time meditating on **Romans 12:13**:

> *"Contribute to the needs of the saints and seek to show hospitality."* (ESV)

What two actions are linked together in this verse? What does it imply about the nature of contributing to needs and showing hospitality? How can this verse encourage a proactive approach to welcoming others?

Now, also read **Hebrews 13:2**:

> *"Do not neglect to show hospitality to strangers, for thereby some have entertained angels unawares."* (ESV)

Why is it important not to "neglect to show hospitality to strangers"? What surprising possibility is mentioned regarding welcoming those we don't know? How does this verse broaden our understanding of whom we are called to welcome?

Guided Reflection:

Write down your reflections on the questions above and your insights from Romans 12:13 and Hebrews 13:2. Consider the people around you, perhaps new colleagues, neighbors, or someone sitting alone at a gathering. What is one practical step you can take this week to extend hospitality and make someone feel truly welcome?

Devotional: Opening Our Hearts and Homes

Hospitality is a powerful way to express God's love. It breaks down barriers, builds bridges, and fosters authentic relationships. It can be as simple as offering a warm smile, striking up a conversation with someone you don't know well, or inviting a new acquaintance for coffee. It might also involve opening your home for a meal, a conversation, or a time of fellowship.

This week let's cultivate a spirit of genuine welcome. Look for opportunities to go out of your way to make others feel seen, valued, and included. This might mean initiating a conversation, inviting someone into your space, or simply paying attention to those who seem overlooked. Remember that showing hospitality is not about impressing others; it's about serving them and demonstrating the inclusive love of Christ.

By intentionally practicing hospitality, we not only bless those we welcome but also enrich our own lives and deepen our understanding of God's heart for all people. It's an active way to live out our faith in community.

Prayer Prompt:

Spend time in prayer asking God for a hospitable heart. Pray for eyes to see those around you who might need a word of welcome or a gesture of inclusion. Ask for courage and wisdom to extend hospitality in ways that honor Him and bless others.

Personal Reflection & Growth Journal

Significant Moments / Insights from This Week's Study

What happened? What was the insight?

_____

_____

_____

_____

_____

Emotional/Spiritual Responses:

_____

_____

_____

_____

_____

Spiritual Insights/Lessons Learned:
- First thoughts:

_____

_____

_____

_____

- New perspectives gained:

_____

_____

_____

_____

- My Response/Action:

_____

_____

_____

_____

What helped me connect with God/grow this ?week?

_____

_____

_____

_____

What hindered my connection/?growth?

_____

_____

_____

_____

Week 36: Encouraging and Building Up Others

In a world that can often be critical or demanding, the power of encouragement is immense. As followers of Christ, we are called to be instruments of God's grace, actively seeking to uplift, affirm, and strengthen those around us. Encouragement is a vital expression of love and a powerful way to build up the body of believers and positively impact our wider communities.

Think about a time when someone's words of encouragement made a significant difference in your life or helped you through a challenging period. What was the impact of their affirmation? Now, consider how you can intentionally be a source of encouragement for others.

Scripture Prompt:

Spend time meditating on **Ephesians 4:29**:

> *"Let no corrupting talk come out of your mouths, but only such as is good for building up, as fits the occasion, that it may give grace to those who hear."* (ESV)

What kind of talk are we commanded to avoid? What kind of speech are we to cultivate instead? What is the purpose of our words ("building up") and their effect ("give grace to those who hear")? How can this verse guide your conversations this week?

Now, also read **1 Thessalonians 5:11**:

> *"Therefore encourage one another and build one another up, just as you are doing."* (ESV)

What is the direct command given regarding our interactions within the community? What does it mean to "build one another up"? How does this verse emphasize that encouragement is a shared responsibility among believers?

Guided Reflection:

Write down your reflections on the questions above and your insights from Ephesians 4:29 and 1 Thessalonians 5:11. Consider specific individuals in your life, such as family members, friends, colleagues, or fellow churchgoers, who might need a word of encouragement this week. What specific words or actions could you offer to build them up?

Devotional: The Gift of Affirmation

Encouragement is a divine gift that breathes life and hope into others. It acknowledges their value, affirms their efforts, and reminds them of God's presence and power in their lives. It's about seeing the potential in others, celebrating their strengths, and gently supporting them through their struggles. This isn't about flattery, but about genuine, heartfelt affirmation rooted in love and truth.

This week let's intentionally look for opportunities to speak life-giving words. Listen attentively for moments when someone expresses doubt, faces a challenge, or feels overlooked. Take a moment to offer sincere praise, express gratitude, or simply remind them of God's faithfulness.

This might involve a verbal affirmation, a thoughtful message, or a specific act of support.

Remember that a single word of encouragement can transform a person's day, strengthen their spirit, and inspire them to persevere. By making encouragement a regular practice, we become channels of God's grace, reflecting His heart that always seeks to uplift and restore.

Prayer Prompt:

Spend time in prayer asking God to give you a heart that is quick to encourage and affirm others. Pray for discernment to know when and how to speak words of life. Ask for the courage to step out and build up those around you, reflecting His love and hope.

Personal Reflection & Growth Journal

Significant Moments / Insights from This Week's Study

What happened? What was the insight?

_____

_____

_____

_____

_____

Emotional/Spiritual Responses:

_____

_____

_____

_____

_____

Spiritual Insights/Lessons Learned:

- First thoughts:

_____

_____

_____

_____

- New perspectives gained:

_____

_____

_____

_____

- My Response/Action:

_____

_____

_____

_____

What helped me connect with God/grow this ?week?

_____

_____

_____

_____

What hindered my connection/?growth?

_____

_____

_____

_____

Week 37: Being a Faithful Friend and Ally

As we continue to explore connecting with others, we delve into the active role of being a faithful friend and ally. This means more than just being present during good times; it involves loyalty, trustworthiness, and standing with others, especially when they face challenges or injustice.

Think about what it truly means to be a loyal friend. Have you had experiences where someone stood by you unconditionally? How did that impact your sense of security and belonging? Consider how you can embody this faithfulness in your own relationships.

Scripture Prompt

Spend time meditating on **Proverbs 18:24**:

"A man of many companions may come to ruin, but there is a friend who sticks closer than a brother." (ESV)

What contrast is drawn here between casual acquaintances and a true friend? What does it mean for a friend to "stick closer than a brother"? How does this proverb highlight the value of deep, faithful friendships?

Now, also read **Galatians 6:2**:

"Bear one another's burdens, and so fulfill the law of Christ." (ESV)

What practical action are we called to perform for one another? What does it mean to "bear one another's burdens"? How does this act of supportive friendship fulfill "the law of Christ," which is often understood as the law of love?

Guided Reflection

Write down your reflections on the questions above and your insights from Proverbs 18:24 and Galatians 6:2. Consider a specific friend or community member whom you can intentionally support or stand with this week. How might you practically "bear their burden" or demonstrate your loyalty?

Devotional: Standing Steadfast with Others

Being a faithful friend and ally means choosing commitment over convenience. It involves listening without judgment, offering practical help when needed, speaking truth in love, and defending those who are vulnerable. This kind of loyalty is a powerful reflection of God's steadfastness towards us. It's about being a safe and reliable presence for others, especially during difficult times.

This week let's look for opportunities to practice faithful friendship. This might involve reaching out to someone who is struggling, advocating for someone who is being unfairly treated, or simply being a consistent and trustworthy presence in someone's life. Think about how you can offer a tangible form of support or encouragement.

Remember that loyalty builds trust, and trust forms the bedrock of strong relationships. By choosing to be faithful friends and allies, we not only strengthen our personal connections but also contribute to a more compassionate and supportive community, mirroring the faithfulness of Christ.

Prayer Prompt

Spend time in prayer asking God for the strength and courage to be a faithful friend and ally to those around you. Pray for discernment to know when and how to bear others' burdens. Ask for a heart that is loyal and trustworthy, reflecting His own steadfast love.

Personal Reflection & Growth Journal

Significant Moments / Insights from This Week's Study

What happened? What was the insight?

_____

_____

_____

_____

_____

Emotional/Spiritual Responses:

_____

_____

_____

_____

Spiritual Insights/Lessons Learned:

• First thoughts:

_____

_____

_____

_____

• New perspectives gained:

_____

_____

_____

- My Response/Action:

_____

_____

_____

_____

What helped me connect with God/grow this ?week?

_____

_____

_____

_____

_____

What hindered my connection/?growth?

_____

_____

_____

_____

Week 38: Practicing Empathy and Understanding

Building strong connections with others requires more than just being present; it demands the ability to step into another person's shoes, to genuinely understand their feelings, and to see the world from their perspective. This is the essence of **empathy**. It's a compassionate response that validates others' experiences, even when we don't fully agree or comprehend.

Think about a time someone truly "got" you, making you feel heard and understood. How did that impact your relationship with them? Now, consider situations where you've struggled to understand another person's viewpoint or emotions. What made it difficult?

Scripture Prompt

Spend time meditating on **Romans 12:15**:

> *"Rejoice with those who rejoice; weep with those who weep."* (ESV)

What does this verse call us to do in relation to others' emotions? What does it mean to truly "rejoice with" or "weep with" someone, rather than just observing their feelings? How does this active participation in others' emotional experiences demonstrate empathy?

Now, also read **1 Peter 3:8**:

> *"Finally, all of you, have unity of mind, sympathy, brotherly love, a tender heart, and a humble mind."* (ESV)

Notice the cluster of qualities mentioned here, including "sympathy" (which is closely related to empathy) and a "tender heart." How do these qualities contribute to our ability to understand and connect with others? Why is a "humble mind" essential for truly understanding another's perspective?

Guided Reflection

Write down your reflections on the questions above and your insights from Romans 12:15 and 1 Peter 3:8. Consider a specific relationship or interaction where you can intentionally practice empathy this week. What questions can you ask to better understand their perspective? How can you genuinely validate their feelings, even if you don't share them?

Devotional: The Bridge of Understanding

Empathy builds a bridge between people, allowing us to connect on a deeper, more meaningful level. It moves beyond just hearing someone's words to truly grasping the emotions and experiences behind them. This doesn't mean we have to agree with every perspective, but it does mean we strive to understand and respond with compassion.

This week let's make a conscious effort to practice empathy in our daily interactions. When someone is speaking, listen not just to respond, but to understand. Ask clarifying questions. Pay attention to non-verbal cues. If someone shares a struggle, resist the urge to immediately offer solutions or advice, and instead, first offer a listening ear and a validating presence. If they share a joy, celebrate genuinely with them.

Remember, empathy is a powerful expression of love. By choosing to understand and connect with others on an emotional level, we reflect the compassionate heart of God, who fully understands our weaknesses and rejoices in our joys.

Prayer Prompt

Spend time in prayer asking God to give you a heart of empathy and a spirit of understanding. Pray for the ability to truly listen and connect with others on a deeper level. Ask for compassion for those who are struggling and genuine joy for those who are celebrating.

Personal Reflection & Growth Journal

Significant Moments / Insights from This Week's Study

What happened? What was the insight?

_____

_____

_____

_____

_____

Emotional/Spiritual Responses:

_____

_____

_____

_____

_____

Spiritual Insights/Lessons Learned:

- First thoughts:

_____

_____

_____

_____

- New perspectives gained:

_____

_____

_____

_____

- My Response/Action:

_____

_____

_____

_____

What helped me connect with God/grow this ?week?

_____

_____

_____

_____

What hindered my connection/?growth?

_____

_____

_____

_____

Week 39: Valuing Diversity and Unity

The world, and indeed our vibrant city, is a tapestry woven with countless different threads – cultures, backgrounds, perspectives, and gifts. As believers, we are called not only to acknowledge this diversity but to truly value it as a reflection of God's creative genius. At the same time, we are commanded to strive for unity in Christ, recognizing that our common faith transcends all differences. Valuing diversity without sacrificing unity, and pursuing unity without erasing unique identities, is a profound expression of godly love.

Think about the various people you encounter in your daily life – perhaps at work, in your neighborhood, or in your spiritual community. How do you respond to those who are different from you? Reflect on the beauty of a diverse group coming together in harmony.

Scripture Prompt

Spend time meditating on **Galatians 3:28**:

> *"There is neither Jew nor Gentile, neither slave nor free, nor is there male and female, for you are all one in Christ Jesus."* (ESV)

What significant distinctions does Paul declare are no longer divisive "in Christ Jesus"? What does this verse teach about the foundation of our unity as believers? How does this spiritual reality challenge any human-made divisions we might hold?

Now, also read **Romans 15:5-7**:

> *"May the God of endurance and encouragement grant you to live in such harmony with one another, in accord with Christ Jesus, that together you may with one voice glorify the God and Father of our Lord Jesus Christ. Therefore welcome one another as Christ has welcomed you, for the glory of God."* (ESV)

What is the ultimate goal of living in "harmony with one another"? How does welcoming each other, despite differences, lead to glorifying God? What is the divine source of this harmony and endurance?

Guided Reflection

Write down your reflections on the questions above and your insights from Galatians 3:28 and Romans 15:5-7. Consider a specific group or individual whose background or perspective is different from your own. How can you actively seek to understand, value, and build bridges with them this week, reflecting the unity we have in Christ?

Devotional: The Richness of God's Design

God delights in variety, and His creation is a testament to His boundless imagination. This diversity extends to humanity, where each person is uniquely gifted and wonderfully made. When we come together as believers, our different strengths, experiences, and cultural expressions contribute to a richer, more complete picture of who God is and how He works. Unity is not uniformity; it's a harmonious blending of distinct parts, all working together for a common purpose – to glorify God.

This week let's intentionally seek to value the diversity within our spiritual community and the wider world. Engage in conversations with those who hold different perspectives. Listen to their stories. Seek to understand their traditions and backgrounds. Look for ways to celebrate the unique contributions each person brings, while always holding fast to the foundational truths that unite us in Christ.

Remember, the Kingdom of God is a place where every tongue, tribe, and nation will worship together. By practicing unity in diversity now, we participate in His glorious eternal plan.

Prayer Prompt

Spend time in prayer thanking God for the beautiful diversity among people. Pray for a heart that genuinely values and appreciates differences. Ask for wisdom to pursue unity within your spiritual community, breaking down barriers and fostering harmony that reflects Christ.

Personal Reflection & Growth Journal

Significant Moments / Insights from This Week's Study

What happened? What was the insight?

_____

_____

_____

_____

_____

Emotional/Spiritual Responses:

_____

_____

_____

_____

_____

Spiritual Insights/Lessons Learned:

- First thoughts:

_____

_____

_____

_____

- New perspectives gained:

_____

_____

_____

_____

- My Response/Action:

_____

_____

_____

_____

What helped me connect with God/grow this ?week?

_____

_____

_____

_____

What hindered my connection/?growth?

_____

_____

_____

_____

Week 40: Being a Good Neighbour and Citizen

Our faith is not just lived within the walls of our homes or places of worship; it is profoundly expressed in how we engage with our broader community and society. Being a good neighbor and a responsible citizen means actively contributing to the well-being of our surroundings, seeking justice, promoting peace, and demonstrating love to all, regardless of their beliefs or backgrounds. This proactive engagement reflects God's heart for

His creation and His desire for shalom (wholeness and peace) in all areas of life.

Think about your immediate neighborhood or the wider societal context you live in. What needs do you observe? How do you currently contribute to the flourishing of your community? Reflect on the ways your faith compels you to be involved beyond your personal circle.

Scripture Prompt

Spend time meditating on **Jeremiah 29:7**:

> *"But seek the welfare of the city where I have sent you into exile, and pray to the Lord on its behalf, for in its welfare you will find your welfare."* (ESV)

Though written in a specific historical context, what timeless principle does this verse convey about our engagement with the place God has put us? What two actions are we called to take for the welfare of our community? How does seeking the welfare of our community ultimately benefit us?

Now, also read **Romans 13:1**:

> *"Let every person be subject to the governing authorities. For there is no authority except from God, and those that exist have been instituted by God."* (ESV)

What general instruction is given regarding governing authorities? What is the divine basis for this instruction? How does this verse inform our approach to our civic responsibilities, such as obeying laws and participating thoughtfully in society?

Guided Reflection

Reflect on the questions above and your insights from Jeremiah 29:7 and Romans 13:1. Consider a specific area in your neighborhood or community where you can actively seek its welfare this week. This might be a small act of kindness, engaging in a local initiative, or simply being a more attentive and caring presence.

Devotional: Contributing to the Common Good

Our faith calls us to be salt and light in the world (Matthew 5:13-16), preserving what is good and illuminating truth. Being a good neighbor and citizen is a practical way to fulfill this calling. It means being mindful of our impact, participating responsibly in civic life, and looking for opportunities to serve beyond our immediate needs. This could involve volunteering, supporting local businesses, respecting public spaces, or simply being a considerate presence where you live and work.

This week let's intentionally consider how we can contribute to the common good. Engage with local news or community concerns. Look for ways to connect with your neighbors. Think about how your actions, even small ones, can foster a more thriving, peaceful, and just environment for everyone.

Remember that God is concerned with justice, peace, and the flourishing of all people. By actively participating as good neighbors and citizens, we become His hands and feet, working towards the redemption and transformation of our world.

Prayer Prompt

Spend time in prayer for your neighborhood and the broader community or city you live in. Pray for its welfare, its leaders, and for justice and peace to prevail. Ask God to show you specific ways you can be a good neighbor and citizen, actively contributing to the common good and reflecting His love.

Personal Reflection & Growth Journal

Significant Moments / Insights from This Week's Study

What happened? What was the insight?

_____

_____

_____

_____

_____

Emotional/Spiritual Responses:

_____

_____

_____

_____

_____

Spiritual Insights/Lessons Learned:

- First thoughts:

_____

_____

_____

_____

- New perspectives gained:

_____

_____

_____

_____

- My Response/Action:

_____

_____

_____

_____

What helped me connect with God/grow this ?week?

_____

_____

_____

_____

What hindered my connection/?growth?

_____

_____

_____

_____

Week 41: Review and Reflection on Connecting with Others

Over the past twelve weeks, we've focused on the vital theme of "Connecting with Others." We've explored the importance of Christian community, building healthy friendships, navigating complex family relationships, extending grace, resolving conflict biblically, practicing empathy, valuing diversity, and being good neighbors and citizens. This week is a dedicated time to pause, reflect, and consider how these principles have shaped our interactions and strengthened our relationships.

Think back over the various relational aspects we've discussed. In which of these areas have you felt challenged to grow? Where have you seen God work in your relationships? What new insights have you gained about reflecting Christ in your connections with others?

Scripture Prompt

Spend time meditating on **John 13:34-35**:

> *"A new commandment I give to you, that you love one another: just as I have loved you, you also are to love one another. By this all people will know that you are my disciples, if you have love for one another."* (ESV)

What is the "new commandment" Jesus gives? What is the standard for this love? What is the intended outcome or testimony of believers loving one another? How does this passage summarize the essence of what we've explored this quarter about connecting with others?

Guided Reflection

Write down your reflections on the questions above and your insights from John 13:34-35. Consider the following:

- Which specific lesson from this quarter on "Connecting with Others" has made the most significant impact on your interactions?

- In what ways have you been able to extend God's love, grace, or understanding to others more intentionally?

- What is one area of your relational life where you sense God is still calling you to greater growth or transformation? What might be the next step?

- How has focusing on these aspects of connection deepened your appreciation for the body of Christ and your role within it?

Devotional: The Ongoing Work of Relationship

Connecting with others in a way that honors God is a lifelong journey, marked by continuous learning, humility, and reliance on the Holy Spirit. The principles we've discussed this quarter are not one-time applications but habits and attitudes to be cultivated over time. Our relationships are living, breathing entities that require ongoing care, attention, and grace.

As we conclude this quarter, let us carry forward the commitment to build healthy relationships, extend genuine welcome, resolve conflict with humility, and be a faithful presence in our communities. May our interactions with family, friends, neighbors, and even strangers be a clear reflection of the love of Christ that lives within us.

May God continue to empower you to love others as He has loved you, drawing them closer to Him through the authenticity and beauty of your connections.

Prayer Prompt

Spend time in prayer thanking God for the gift of relationships and for the growth you've experienced in connecting with others this quarter. Pray for a heart that continuously seeks to love others as Christ loves. Ask for His guidance and strength to navigate all your relationships in a way that brings Him glory.

Personal Reflection & Growth Journal

Significant Moments / Insights from This Week's Study

What happened? What was the insight?

_____

_____

_____

_____

_____

Emotional/Spiritual Responses:

_____

_____

_____

_____

Spiritual Insights/Lessons Learned:

• First thoughts:

_____

_____

_____

- New perspectives gained:

_____

_____

_____

_____

- My Response/Action:

_____

_____

_____

_____

What helped me connect with God/grow this ?week?

_____

_____

_____

_____

What hindered my connection/?growth?

_____

_____

_____

_____

IV. Quarter 4: Living with Purpose (Weeks 42-52) -
Theme: Discovering and Fulfilling God's Calling

Week 42: Living with Purpose

Having spent time deepening our knowledge of God and learning to live out our faith in our relationships, we now move into a profound exploration of **purpose**. This quarter, "Living with Purpose," invites us to consider God's unique calling for each of us. It's about discovering how our gifts, passions, and experiences can align with His greater plan for us and for the world around us.

Think about moments when you've felt a strong sense of meaning or direction in your life. What was happening? Reflect on the longing we all have to know why we are here and to make a meaningful difference.

Scripture Prompt

Spend time meditating on **Ephesians 2:10**:

"For we are his workmanship, created in Christ Jesus for good works, which God prepared beforehand, that we should walk in them." (ESV)

What does it mean that we are God's "workmanship"? What is the purpose for which we were "created in Christ Jesus"? How does the phrase "God prepared beforehand" affect your understanding of your own life's journey? What does it imply about the intentionality of God's plan for you?

Guided Reflection

Use your journal or a notebook to record your reflections on the questions above and your insights from Ephesians 2:10. Consider your life thus far. Can you identify any "good works" that God seems to have prepared for you, even if you didn't recognize them as such at the time? How might embracing this truth influence your perspective on your future?

Devotional: Called to Live Intentionally

Every person is uniquely designed by God with specific gifts, talents, and a story to tell. Our purpose isn't something we create out of thin air; it's something we discover as we draw closer to our Creator. It's about aligning our lives with His will, using what He's given us to serve Him and others. This quarter will help us explore how our daily choices, our careers, our relationships, and our passions can all be avenues through which we fulfill God's calling.

This week, begin to approach your life with an attitude of curiosity and surrender. Ask God to reveal His purposes for you, starting with the very next steps. Pay attention to what breaks your heart, what ignites your passion, and what unique abilities you possess. These can often be clues to where God is calling you to walk in the "good works" He has prepared.

Remember, living with purpose brings profound joy and fulfillment. It's not about perfection, but about faithfully seeking and responding to God's lead, knowing that every act done in His name has eternal significance.

Prayer Prompt

Spend time in prayer asking God to reveal His purpose for your life. Pray for clarity, direction, and a heart that is eager to walk in the good works He has prepared for you. Ask for a renewed sense of meaning and intention in your daily tasks.

Personal Reflection & Growth Journal

Significant Moments / Insights from This Week's Study

What happened? What was the insight?

_____

_____

_____

_____

_____

Emotional/Spiritual Responses:

_____

_____

_____

_____

Spiritual Insights/Lessons Learned:

- First thoughts:

_____

_____

_____

- New perspectives gained:

_____

_____

_____

- My Response/Action:

_____

_____

_____

What helped me connect with God/grow this ?week?

_____

_____

_____

_____

_____

What hindered my connection/?growth?

_____

_____

_____

_____

_____

Week 43: Discovering Your Gifts and Talents

Every individual is uniquely wired by God, endowed with a distinct set of gifts, talents, and abilities. These are not random; they are intentional tools given to us to fulfill His purposes and contribute to the flourishing of the world around us. Discovering and understanding your unique gifting is a crucial step in aligning your life with God's calling and living with a profound sense of purpose. Whether your strengths lie in creativity, leadership, compassion, practical skills, or deep insight, each plays a vital role in the tapestry of human endeavor.

Think about what comes naturally to you, what you enjoy doing, or what others consistently affirm in you. Reflect on areas where you feel a sense of competence or where you instinctively know how to help.

Scripture Prompt

Spend time meditating on **1 Corinthians 12:4-7**:

> *"Now there are varieties of gifts, but the same Spirit; and there are varieties of service, but the same Lord; and there are varieties of activities, but it is the same God who empowers them all in everyone. To each is given the manifestation of the Spirit for the common good."* (ESV)

What does this passage emphasize about the *source* of our gifts and talents? What is the ultimate *purpose* for which these gifts are given? How does this verse highlight the diversity within unity when it comes to giftedness?

Now, also read **Romans 12:6-8**:

> *"Having gifts that differ according to the grace given to us, let us use them: if prophecy, in proportion to our faith; if service, in our serving; the one who teaches, in his teaching; the one who exhorts, in his exhortation; the one who contributes, in generosity; the one who leads, with zeal; the one who does acts of mercy, with cheerfulness."* (ESV)

This passage lists various gifts. What is the overarching instruction given for each of them? What does it imply about the importance of actively *using* the gifts we've been given, rather than neglecting them?

Guided Reflection

Write down your reflections on the questions above and your insights from 1 Corinthians 12:4-7 and Romans 12:6-8. List some of the gifts, talents, or strengths you believe God has given you. How have you used them recently? How might you use them more intentionally for the "common good" this week?

Devotional: Unleashing Your God-Given Potential

Discovering your gifts isn't just about identifying what you're good at; it's about recognizing how God has uniquely equipped you to bring His light into the world. Sometimes our gifts are obvious, honed through education or practice. Other times, they are subtle inclinations or burdens we feel for specific needs. The journey of purpose begins by acknowledging that you are wonderfully made and uniquely endowed.

This week, commit to a deeper exploration of your gifts. Pay attention to moments when you feel most alive and useful. Ask trusted friends or mentors what strengths they see in you. Reflect on past experiences where you made a difference. Most importantly, ask God to reveal His specific design for you and how He wants you to use it.

Remember, every gift, no matter how seemingly small, is significant in God's eyes. By embracing and utilizing our God-given abilities, we participate in His ongoing work and experience the profound joy of living out His intended purpose for our lives.

Prayer Prompt

Spend time in prayer thanking God for the unique gifts and talents He has given you. Pray for clarity and discernment to fully understand how you are wired. Ask for courage and opportunities to faithfully use your gifts for His glory and for the benefit of others.

Personal Reflection & Growth Journal

Significant Moments / Insights from This Week's Study

What happened? What was the insight?

_____

_____

_____

_____

Emotional/Spiritual Responses:

_____

_____

_____

_____

Spiritual Insights/Lessons Learned:
- First thoughts:

_____

_____

_____

_____

- New perspectives gained:

_____

_____

_____

_____

- My Response/Action:

_____

_____

_____

_____

What helped me connect with God/grow this ?week?

_____

_____

_____

_____

What hindered my connection/?growth?

_____

_____

_____

_____

Week 44: Serving God and Others

Having recognized our unique gifts and talents, the next step in living with purpose is to actively deploy them in service to God and others. Our purpose is rarely found in isolation; it flourishes in the context of contributing to something larger than ourselves. Whether it's through grand gestures or daily acts of kindness, serving is the tangible expression of our faith and a powerful way to reflect God's love to the world, impacting lives right here in our vibrant communities.

Think about a time when you served someone else, and it brought you unexpected joy or fulfillment. What was that experience like? Consider the various needs you see around you, both big and small, and how your gifts might address them.

Scripture Prompt

Spend time meditating on **Mark 10:45**:

"For even the Son of Man came not to be served but to serve, and to give his life as a ransom for many." (ESV)

What does Jesus' own example teach us about the essence of true greatness and purpose? How does His sacrificial service inform our understanding of what it means to serve others?

Now, also read **Matthew 25:40**:

"And the King will answer them, 'Truly, I say to you, as you did it to one of the least of these my brothers, you did it to me.'" (ESV)

What profound connection does Jesus make between serving "the least of these" and serving Him directly? How does this elevate the significance of every act of service, no matter how small?

Guided Reflection

Write down your answers for the questions above and your insights from Mark 10:45 and Matthew 25:40. Identify specific areas or needs in your life, church, or community where you could offer your gifts in service this week. Consider both formal and informal opportunities.

Devotional: The Joy of a Serving Heart

Serving God and others is not a burdensome duty, but a privilege and a pathway to profound joy. When we use our time, energy, and gifts to meet the needs of those around us, we step into the very heart of God, who is Himself a servant. It's in giving that we truly receive, and in pouring ourselves out for others that we find our lives filled with meaning.

This week let's intentionally look for opportunities to serve. This might involve volunteering your time in a local initiative, offering practical help to a friend or neighbor, sharing your skills at your church, or simply being attentive to moments where a kind word or a listening ear is needed. Don't underestimate the power of seemingly small acts; they can have immense impact.

Remember that every act of service, done with a sincere heart for God, has eternal value. By cultivating a serving heart, we not only live out our purpose but also become tangible expressions of Christ's love in a world desperately in need.

Prayer Prompt

Spend time in prayer asking God to give you a servant's heart and to open your eyes to the needs around you. Pray for wisdom to know how best to use your gifts in service to Him and to others. Ask for the joy that comes from generous giving of yourself.

Personal Reflection & Growth Journal

Significant Moments / Insights from This Week's Study

What happened? What was the insight?

_____

_____

_____

_____

_____

Emotional/Spiritual Responses:

_____

_____

_____

_____

_____

Spiritual Insights/Lessons Learned:

- First thoughts:

_____

_____

_____

_____

- New perspectives gained:

_____

_____

_____

_____

- My Response/Action:

_____

_____

_____

_____

What helped me connect with God/grow this ?week?

_____

_____

_____

_____

What hindered my connection/?growth?

_____

_____

_____

_____

Week 45: Cultivating a Kingdom Mindset

As we deepen our understanding of purpose and service, it's essential to cultivate a "Kingdom mindset." This means seeing beyond our immediate circumstances and personal aspirations to God's overarching plan for humanity and the world. It's about understanding that our individual purpose is intrinsically linked to His larger Kingdom purpose - bringing justice, love, and redemption to every sphere of life. This perspective shifts our focus from mere self-fulfillment to actively participating in God's ongoing work, impacting our community and beyond.

Think about how your daily decisions are influenced by your understanding of God's Kingdom. Do you consider the broader implications of your actions? Reflect on the difference it makes when you view your life not just through a personal lens, but through the lens of God's redemptive plan.

Scripture Prompt

Spend time meditating on **Matthew 6:33**:

> *"But seek first the kingdom of God and his righteousness, and all these things will be added to you."* (ESV)

What is the primary pursuit Jesus instructs us to have? What does it mean to "seek first the kingdom of God and his righteousness"? What promise accompanies this pursuit? How does this verse guide our priorities in living a purposeful life?

Now, also read **Romans 14:17**:

> *"For the kingdom of God is not a matter of eating and drinking but of righteousness and peace and joy in the Holy Spirit."* (ESV)

What does this verse clarify the Kingdom of God *is not* about? What are the true characteristics of the Kingdom of God? How does understanding these characteristics shape our pursuit of purpose and influence our interactions in the world?

Guided Reflection

Write down your reflections on the questions above and your insights from Matthew 6:33 and Romans 14:17. Consider a specific area of your life: your work, your finances, your hobbies, or your relationships. How can you more intentionally align this area with a Kingdom mindset this week, prioritizing righteousness, peace, and joy in the Holy Spirit?

Devotional: Living for a Greater Story

A Kingdom mindset transforms how we view our lives. It liberates us from the endless pursuit of personal gain and invites us into a grander narrative – God's story of redemption. When we truly grasp that we are co-laborers with Him, every task, every conversation, and every decision can become an act of worship and a contribution to His eternal purposes. This perspective helps us navigate challenges with resilience and celebrate successes with gratitude, knowing that all things are ultimately for His glory.

This week, challenge yourself to think with a Kingdom mindset. When you're making a decision, ask, "How does this align with God's righteousness? Will it bring peace? Will it foster joy in the Holy Spirit?" Look for opportunities to act justly, love mercy, and walk humbly, knowing these are expressions of the Kingdom here on Earth. Consider the specific challenges or injustices in your community or in the wider world and prayerfully consider how God might want you to respond within His Kingdom framework.

Remember, living with a Kingdom mindset allows us to experience profound fulfillment, knowing that our lives are part of something eternal and infinitely meaningful. It's an invitation to join God in His ongoing work of bringing His reign to bear on every corner of creation.

Prayer Prompt

Spend time in prayer asking God to give you a deeper understanding and a consistent application of a Kingdom mindset. Pray for your eyes to see His purposes in the world and for your heart to be aligned with His righteousness, peace, and joy. Ask for boldness to live for His Kingdom above all else.

Personal Reflection & Growth Journal

Significant Moments / Insights from This Week's Study

What happened? What was the insight?

_____

_____

_____

_____

_____

Emotional/Spiritual Responses:

_____

_____

_____

_____

_____

Spiritual Insights/Lessons Learned:

- First thoughts:

_____

_____

_____

_____

- New perspectives gained:

_____

_____

_____

_____

- My Response/Action:

_____

_____

_____

_____

What helped me connect with God/grow this ?week?

_____

_____

_____

_____

What hindered my connection/?growth?

_____

_____

_____

_____

Week 46: Overcoming Obstacles with Faith

Living a purposeful life, aligned with God's calling, doesn't mean the absence of challenges. In fact, pursuing God's will often brings its own set of obstacles, setbacks, and moments of doubt. However, our faith provides the foundation and strength to navigate these difficulties, seeing them not as roadblocks to our purpose, but as opportunities for growth, deeper reliance on God, and clearer revelation of His power.

Think about a significant obstacle you've faced in the past. How did you respond? Did your faith play a role in overcoming it? Reflect on any current challenges that feel daunting, and consider how a faith-filled perspective might change your approach.

Scripture Prompt

Spend time meditating on **Philippians 4:13**:

> *"I can do all things through him who strengthens me."* (ESV)

What powerful affirmation does Paul make in this verse? What is the source of this strength? How does this verse empower us to face difficulties when pursuing God's calling?

Now, also read **Romans 8:28**:

> *"And we know that for those who love God all things work together for good, for those who are called according to his purpose."* (ESV)

What profound assurance is given to those who love God and are called according to His purpose? Does "all things" imply the absence of difficulty, or something deeper? How does this verse encourage perseverance and trust in God's sovereignty even amidst setbacks?

Guided Reflection

Reflect on the questions above and your insights from Philippians 4:13 and Romans 8:28. Identify a specific obstacle (personal, professional, or spiritual) you are currently facing or anticipate. How can you apply the truths from these scriptures to that situation this week? What specific action can you take, trusting in God's strength and purpose?

Devotional: Faith as Our Anchor in the Storm

Obstacles are an inherent part of the human journey, but for those living with purpose in Christ, they are not insurmountable. Our faith acts as an anchor, holding us steady when the winds of adversity blow. It reminds us that God is bigger than any problem, that His strength is made perfect in our weakness, and that He is always working for our good and His glory, even when circumstances seem chaotic. Overcoming with faith isn't about wishing problems away, but facing them with courage, resilience, and a deep trust in God's unfailing presence and power.

This week, when you encounter a challenge, pause and remember God's promises. Instead of succumbing to fear or discouragement, actively seek His perspective. Ask Him for the strength, wisdom, and creativity to navigate the situation. Lean into your community for support and prayer.

See if this obstacle might be a divinely orchestrated opportunity for you to grow, learn, or witness to God's faithfulness.

Remember, every obstacle overcome by faith strengthens your character and deepens your testimony. You are not alone in this journey; the God who called you is faithful to equip and sustain you through every trial, ultimately working all things for good towards His purposes.

Prayer Prompt

Spend time in prayer for any specific obstacles or challenges you are currently facing. Ask God for unwavering faith to overcome them. Pray for His strength to be evident in your weakness, for His wisdom to guide your steps, and for the peace that comes from trusting in His ultimate plan.

Personal Reflection & Growth Journal

Significant Moments / Insights from This Week's Study

What happened? What was the insight?

_____

_____

_____

_____

Emotional/Spiritual Responses:

_____

_____

_____

_____

Spiritual Insights/Lessons Learned:
- First thoughts:

_____

_____

_____

_____

- New perspectives gained:

_____

_____

_____

_____

- My Response/Action:

_____

_____

_____

_____

What helped me connect with God/grow this ?week?

_____

_____

_____

_____

What hindered my connection/?growth?

_____

_____

_____

_____

Week 47: Stewarding Your Resources for God's Kingdom

Living with purpose extends to how we manage every aspect of our lives, including finances and possessions. Stewarding our resources for God's Kingdom means recognizing that everything we have is ultimately a gift from Him, entrusted to us to be used for His glory and the advancement of His purposes. It's about prioritizing generosity, living responsibly, and making wise choices with what God has given us, acknowledging that we are managers, not owners. This applies whether we are considering our personal budget or contributing to initiatives that uplift our communities.

Think about your current approach to managing your resources. Do you view them as solely yours, or as gifts entrusted to you by God? Reflect on how your financial and material choices align with your faith and your sense of purpose.

Scripture Prompt

Spend time meditating on **2 Corinthians 9:7-8**:

> *"Each one must give as he has decided in his heart, not reluctantly or under compulsion, for God loves a cheerful giver. And God is able to make all grace abound to you, so that having all sufficiency in all things at all times, you may abound in every good work."* (ESV)

What attitude should characterize our giving? What promise is given to the cheerful giver, and how does it relate to "every good work"? How does this passage encourage generous stewardship as a pathway to fulfilling purpose?

Now, also read **Matthew 6:19-21**:

> *"Do not lay up for yourselves treasures on earth, where moth and rust destroy and where thieves break in and steal, but lay up for yourselves treasures in heaven, where neither moth nor rust destroys and where thieves do not break in and steal. For where your treasure is, there your heart will be also."* (ESV)

What contrast does Jesus draw between earthly and heavenly treasures? Where does He say our "heart will be" in relation to our treasure? How does this teaching guide our perspective on accumulating wealth and possessions, and how does it relate to living purposefully for God's Kingdom?

Guided Reflection

Write down your reflections on the questions above and your insights from 2 Corinthians 9:7-8 and Matthew 6:19-21. Consider your current financial habits and use of possessions. What is one practical step you can take this week to more intentionally **steward your resources** for God's Kingdom, whether through giving, responsible spending, or wise saving?

Devotional: Using What We Have for Eternal Impact

Stewardship is a powerful expression of our trust in God and our commitment to His Kingdom. It's not just about tithing or giving financially, though those are important. It's about recognizing that every rand, every possession, every skill, and every opportunity is a tool God can use if we surrender it to Him. When we manage our resources wisely and generously, we become active participants in God's redemptive work, supporting ministries, aiding those in need, and investing in initiatives that bring about lasting change.

This week, take time to review your financial and material resources with a **Kingdom mindset**. Ask God to show you how you can use what you have to further His purposes. This might involve setting a budget that allows for generous giving, making intentional decisions about your purchases, or finding ways to use your possessions to bless others. Remember, even small acts of faithful stewardship can have significant eternal impact.

By entrusting our resources to God, we free ourselves from the anxieties of accumulation and step into the joy of participating in His abundant provision and eternal plans.

Prayer Prompt

Spend time in prayer thanking God for His provision and for entrusting you with resources. Pray for wisdom and discipline to be a faithful steward of everything you have. Ask for a generous heart that desires to use your resources for His Kingdom purposes and for the good of others.

Personal Reflection & Growth Journal

Significant Moments / Insights from This Week's Study

What happened? What was the insight?

_____
_____
_____
_____

Emotional/Spiritual Responses:

_____
_____
_____
_____

Spiritual Insights/Lessons Learned:

- First thoughts:

_____
_____
_____

- New perspectives gained:

_____
_____
_____

- My Response/Action:

_____
_____
_____

What helped me connect with God/grow this ?week?

_____

_____

_____

_____

_____

What hindered my connection/?growth?

_____

_____

_____

_____

_____

Week 48: Living with Endurance and Long-Term Vision

Fulfilling God's purpose for our lives is rarely a short-term sprint; it's a marathon that requires sustained effort, perseverance, and a steadfast gaze towards the future. A life of purpose is built day by day, choice by choice, often demanding endurance through periods of waiting, challenge, or seemingly small progress. Cultivating a long-term vision, grounded in God's faithfulness, enables us to remain steadfast, even when the immediate path is unclear.

Think about areas in your life where you've had to show remarkable endurance to achieve a goal. What kept you going? Reflect on any areas where you feel discouraged or impatient in your pursuit of purpose, and consider the role of a long-term perspective.

Scripture Prompt

Spend time meditating on **Hebrews 12:1-2**:

> *"Therefore, since we are surrounded by so great a cloud of witnesses, let us also lay aside every weight, and sin which clings so closely, and let us run with endurance the race that is set before us, looking to Jesus, the founder and perfecter of our faith, who for the joy that was set before him endured the cross, despising the shame, and is seated at the right hand of the throne of God."* (ESV)

What imagery is used to describe the Christian life and our pursuit of purpose? What are we encouraged to "lay aside"? What is the central focus or model for our endurance? How does Jesus' own endurance inspire us to live with long-term vision?

Now, also read **Proverbs 29:18 (KJV or similar for "vision")**:

> *"Where there is no prophetic vision the people cast off restraint, but blessed is he who keeps the law."* (ESJV or preferred translation like NASB "revelation")

While "prophetic vision" can mean direct revelation, it broadly speaks to a clear sense of divine purpose or direction. What is the consequence when there is no such vision? What positive outcome comes from holding onto and living by God's revealed will? How does a clear, long-term vision provide direction and guard against aimlessness?

Guided Reflection

Write down your reflections on the questions above and your insights from Hebrews 12:1-2 and Proverbs 29:18. Consider your personal purpose journey. What specific "weights or sins" might be hindering your endurance? What long-term vision for your life or your contribution to God's Kingdom keeps you motivated through challenges?

Devotional: The Steadfast Pursuit of Calling

Living with endurance means committing to God's calling even when results aren't immediately visible, or the path is arduous. It's understanding that growth, transformation, and impact often happen incrementally, not instantaneously. A long-term vision, rooted in God's unchanging character and promises, allows us to persist through setbacks, knowing that His timing is perfect and His ultimate plan will prevail. It liberates us from the tyranny of immediate gratification and anchors us in eternal significance.

This week, intentionally cultivate a spirit of endurance and a long-term vision. When you feel impatient or discouraged, remind yourself of God's faithfulness throughout history and in your own life. Re-read scriptures that speak to perseverance and God's ultimate victory. Identify one area where you need more endurance and focus on taking small, consistent steps forward, trusting that God is at work, even when you can't see the full picture.

Remember, the greatest impact often comes from sustained faithfulness. By running with endurance and holding onto God's vision, you are positioning yourself to fulfill the deep and lasting purposes He has for your life, contributing to His eternal Kingdom.

Prayer Prompt

Spend time in prayer asking God for strength and endurance to run the race He has set before you. Pray for a clear, long-term vision for your purpose that keeps you focused amidst distractions and challenges. Ask for patience and trust in His perfect timing.

Personal Reflection & Growth Journal

Significant Moments / Insights from This Week's Study

What happened? What was the insight?

_____

_____

_____

_____

_____

Emotional/Spiritual Responses:

_____

_____

_____

_____

_____

Spiritual Insights/Lessons Learned:
- First thoughts:

_____

_____

_____

_____

- New perspectives gained:

_____

_____

_____

_____

- My Response/Action:

_____

_____

_____

_____

What helped me connect with God/grow this ?week?

_____

_____

_____

_____

What hindered my connection/?growth?

_____

_____

_____

_____

Week 49: Leaving a Godly Legacy

As we journey through "Living with Purpose," we come to reflect on the lasting impact of our lives – the legacy we leave behind. A godly legacy isn't necessarily about fame or wealth, but about the enduring influence of our faith, character, and service on future generations and the world around us. It's about living in such a way that our purpose continues to bear fruit long after we are gone, sowing seeds of righteousness and truth that will bless others. In a land with a rich history and a vibrant future like South Africa, thinking about legacy connects us deeply to the past and our responsibility for what lies ahead.

Think about individuals who have left a positive, godly legacy in your life or in history. What characteristics defined their impact? Reflect on what kind of spiritual, relational, or societal impact you hope to leave, guided by your faith.

Scripture Prompt

Spend time meditating on **Psalm 78:4**:

> *"We will not hide them from their children, but tell to the coming generation the glorious deeds of the Lord, and his might, and the wonders that he has done."* (ESV)

What is the responsibility of one generation towards the next? What specific "deeds of the Lord" are meant to be passed on? How does this verse highlight the intergenerational aspect of godly legacy?

Now, also read **Hebrews 11:4**:

> *"By faith Abel offered to God a more acceptable sacrifice than Cain, through which he was commended as righteous, God commending him by accepting his gifts. And through his faith, though he died, he still speaks."* (ESV)

What was the defining characteristic of Abel's life and offering? How did his faith continue to "speak" even after his death? What does this imply about the lasting power of a life lived by faith, regardless of its length or public recognition?

Guided Reflection

Reflect on the questions above and your insights from Psalm 78:4 and Hebrews 11:4. Consider the spheres of influence God has given you (family, friends, workplace, community). What specific spiritual truths, values, or acts of service do you want to intentionally cultivate and pass on to those who come after you?

Devotional: Living with Tomorrow in Mind

A godly legacy is built not by grand plans alone, but by consistent, faithful living in the present. It's woven into the fabric of our daily choices: the words we speak, the integrity we uphold, the love we show, the compassion we extend, and the wisdom we share. It's about investing in people and principles that outlast us, understanding that our purpose has an eternal dimension. The impact we have often ripples far beyond what we can immediately see or measure.

This week, approach your days with an awareness of the legacy you are building. Consider how your actions and choices today might influence tomorrow. This could involve mentoring someone younger, investing in a cause that promotes justice, teaching biblical truths to your children or spiritual children, or simply living with such authentic faith that it inspires others. Think about the values you want to be remembered for and actively seek to embody them.

Remember, every life lived for Christ leaves a lasting imprint. By intentionally pursuing God's purpose and faithfully stewarding the influence He gives us, we contribute to a legacy that glorifies Him and blesses generations to come.

Prayer Prompt

Spend time in prayer asking God to help you live with an eternal perspective and to build a godly legacy. Pray for wisdom to know how to invest your life in ways that will have lasting spiritual impact. Ask for a heart that desires to bless future generations and to reflect Christ's enduring love through your life.

Personal Reflection & Growth Journal

Significant Moments / Insights from This Week's Study

What happened? What was the insight?

_____

_____

_____

_____

_____

Emotional/Spiritual Responses:

_____

_____

_____

_____

_____

Spiritual Insights/Lessons Learned:

- First thoughts:

_____

_____

_____

_____

- New perspectives gained:

_____

_____

_____

_____

- My Response/Action:

_____

_____

_____

_____

What helped me connect with God/grow this ?week?

_____

_____

_____

_____

_____

What hindered my connection/?growth?

_____

_____

_____

_____

_____

Week 50: Embracing Continuous Growth and Future Purpose

As we draw closer to the end of our annual journey, it's crucial to understand that living with purpose is not a destination we arrive at and then cease to develop. Instead, it is a dynamic, lifelong process of continuous growth, adaptation, and discovery. God's calling unfolds in seasons, often revealing new facets of our purpose as we mature in faith and experience. Embracing this ongoing journey allows us to remain flexible, open to His leading, and ready for the next steps in our purposeful lives, much like how the landscapes around us change with the seasons, revealing new beauty.

Think about how you have grown and changed over the past year, or even over your lifetime. What new understandings or challenges have shaped your path? Reflect on the idea that God's purpose for you might evolve and expand.

Scripture Prompt

Spend time meditating on **Philippians 3:13-14**:

> *"Brothers, I do not consider that I have made it my own. But one thing I do: forgetting what lies behind and straining forward to what lies ahead, I press on toward the goal for the prize of the upward call of God in Christ Jesus."* (ESV)

What attitude does Paul express about his past accomplishments or failures? What is his singular focus? How does this verse encourage a forward-looking perspective in our pursuit of purpose, rather than dwelling on the past?

Now, also read **Proverbs 16:9**:

> *"The heart of man plans his way, but the Lord establishes his steps."* (ESV)

What does this proverb say about human planning? What is God's role in our journey and plans? How does acknowledging God's sovereignty encourage both our active planning and our openness to His divine redirection in our purpose?

Guided Reflection

Reflect on the questions above and your insights from Philippians 3:13-14 and Proverbs 16:9. Consider an area of your life where you sense a need for continued growth. What new skills, knowledge, or spiritual disciplines might God be inviting you to explore for future purpose?

Devotional: The Unfolding Tapestry of God's Plan

God's purpose for us is often like a tapestry, where each thread of our past, present, and future is intricately woven together. We may only see a small section at a time, but with each new season and every step of growth, more of the beautiful design is revealed. Embracing continuous growth means maintaining a posture of learning, humility, and responsiveness to the Holy Spirit. It means being willing to adapt, to shed old ways of thinking, and to step into new challenges as God leads.

This week, intentionally reflect on the journey you've taken so far this year. What lessons have you learned? What new strengths have you discovered? As you look forward, hold your plans loosely, trusting that God is establishing your steps. Be open to new opportunities for service, learning, or contribution that may not fit your current expectations.

Remember, the God who began a good work in you will carry it on to completion (Philippians 1:6). Your purpose is an unfolding story, and each step of growth prepares you for the next chapter of living a life fully devoted to Him.

Prayer Prompt

Spend time in prayer thanking God for the journey of growth and purpose. Pray for a heart that is eager to learn and adapt, and for open hands to receive whatever new assignments or opportunities He has for you. Ask for clarity and boldness as you step into the next season of His unfolding plan for your life.

Personal Reflection & Growth Journal

Significant Moments / Insights from This Week's Study

What happened? What was the insight?

_____

_____

_____

_____

_____

Emotional/Spiritual Responses:

_____

_____

_____

_____

_____

Spiritual Insights/Lessons Learned:

- First thoughts:

_____

_____

_____

_____

- New perspectives gained:

_____

_____

_____

_____

- My Response/Action:

_____

_____

_____

_____

What helped me connect with God/grow this ?week?

_____

_____

_____

_____

What hindered my connection/?growth?

_____

_____

_____

_____

Week 51: Gratitude and Celebration in Purpose

As we approach the culmination of our annual journey, it's vital to pause and cultivate a spirit of **gratitude** and **celebration** in our purposeful living. True purpose isn't just about striving; it's also about acknowledging God's faithfulness in our lives and His work through us. Taking time to celebrate milestones, no matter how small, and to express heartfelt thanks for His guidance and provision, strengthens our faith and energises us for the path ahead. This practice allows us to truly appreciate the beauty of the journey and the blessings along the way.

Think back over the entire year of this devotional journey. What are some specific instances where you've seen God's hand at work in your life? What achievements, insights, or moments of growth are you particularly grateful for?

Scripture Prompt

Spend time meditating on **Psalm 100:4-5**:

"Enter his gates with thanksgiving, and his courts with praise! Give thanks to him; bless his name! For the Lord is good; his steadfast love endures forever, and his faithfulness to all generations." (ESV)

What actions are we encouraged to take when approaching God? What are the specific reasons given for giving thanks and praise? How does remembering God's goodness, steadfast love, and faithfulness encourage a spirit of gratitude in our purposeful lives?

Now, also read **1 Thessalonians 5:18**:

"give thanks in all circumstances; for this is the will of God in Christ Jesus for you." (ESV)

What is the scope of this instruction regarding thanksgiving? What significant statement is made about its importance? How does practicing gratitude in *all* circumstances, even challenges, align with fulfilling God's will and purpose?

Guided Reflection

Write down your reflections on the questions above and your insights from Psalm 100:4-5 and 1 Thessalonians 5:18. Identify three specific things you are grateful for from this past year related to your purpose, growth, or connections with others. How can you intentionally celebrate or express this gratitude to God and to others this week?

Devotional: The Power of a Thankful Heart

Gratitude shifts our perspective from what is lacking to what has been given. Celebration allows us to acknowledge God's active presence and power in our lives, reinforcing our trust in Him for the future. In our pursuit of purpose, it's easy to focus only on what's next, or what still needs to be done. However, pausing to express thanks and celebrate empowers us, deepens our joy, and confirms that our efforts are not in vain, but are part of a larger, divinely orchestrated plan.

This week, intentionally practice gratitude. Keep a gratitude journal, listing specific blessings related to your purposeful journey. Take time to verbally thank God for His guidance. Share stories of His faithfulness with trusted friends or family. Consider a small, personal celebration for a milestone reached or a challenge overcome. This isn't about pride, but about recognizing God's grace at work in and through you.

Remember, a thankful heart is a magnet for more blessings. By embracing gratitude and celebration, you not only honor God but also cultivate a spirit of joy that sustains you in your ongoing pursuit of His purpose.

Prayer Prompt

Spend time in prayer expressing deep gratitude to God for His faithfulness throughout the year and for the purpose He has revealed in your life. Thank Him for specific ways He has led, provided, and used you. Pray for a heart that is always quick to give thanks and to celebrate His goodness.

Personal Reflection & Growth Journal

Significant Moments / Insights from This Week's Study

What happened? What was the insight?

_____

_____

_____

_____

_____

Emotional/Spiritual Responses:

_____

_____

_____

_____

_____

Spiritual Insights/Lessons Learned:

- First thoughts:

_____

_____

_____

_____

- New perspectives gained:

_____

_____

_____

_____

- My Response/Action:

_____

_____

_____

_____

What helped me connect with God/grow this ?week?

_____

_____

_____

_____

What hindered my connection/?growth?

_____

_____

_____

_____

Week 52: Annual Review and Looking Ahead

This week marks the culmination of our year-long devotional journey. We've explored God's unchanging nature, the practical application of our faith in daily life, the beauty of connecting with others, and the profound journey of discovering and fulfilling God's purpose. This final week is a dedicated time for holistic review, to celebrate God's faithfulness throughout the entire year, and to prayerfully look ahead to what He has in store. It's a chance to consolidate your learnings and consider how you'll continue to walk in a deeper relationship with Him in the coming year.

Think back over the past 51 weeks. What was the most significant spiritual insight you gained? How has your understanding of God, yourself, and your relationships evolved? What are you most grateful for as you reflect on this journey?

Scripture Prompt

Spend time meditating on **Psalm 90:12**:

> *"So teach us to number our days that we may get a heart of wisdom."* (ESV)

What does "numbering our days" imply about our approach to time? What is the desired outcome of this practice? How does reflecting on the past year, in light of this verse, contribute to gaining a "heart of wisdom" for the future?

Now, also read **Philippians 1:6**:

> *"And I am sure of this, that he who began a good work in you will bring it to completion at the day of Jesus Christ."* (ESV)

What assurance does this verse offer regarding God's work in your life? What does it mean that God will "bring it to completion"? How does this promise empower you as you look ahead to continuous growth and purpose in the coming year?

Guided Reflection

Write down your reflections on the questions above and your insights from Psalm 90:12 and Philippians 1:6. Take time to review your journal entries from throughout the year. Consider the following:

- What are the top three spiritual truths or practices that had the most significant impact on you this year?

- In what specific area(s) of your life (e.g., relationship with God, living out faith, connecting with others, purpose) did you experience the most growth?

- What is one area you feel God is highlighting for continued focus and deeper spiritual growth in the upcoming year?

- As you look ahead, what specific prayer or intention do you want to carry with you into the new year, trusting God's faithfulness?

Devotional: A Year of Grace, A Future of Promise

Completing a year-long journey like this is a testament to God's grace and your perseverance. It's a moment to acknowledge how far you've come, the lessons you've learned, and the ways God has faithfully met you in each week's exploration. The purpose of this final review isn't just to reminisce, but to solidify the foundations laid and to anticipate the ongoing work of God in your life.

As you step into a new season, remember that God's work in you is continuous. He is not done shaping you, revealing Himself to you, or using you for His Kingdom purposes. Approach the coming year with a sense of anticipation, a heart open to His leading, and a commitment to applying the truths you've learned. Carry forward the disciplines that have brought you closer to Him and be willing to embrace new challenges and opportunities for growth.

May this review be a moment of deep gratitude, renewed commitment, and joyful expectation for all that God will do in and through you in the days ahead.

Prayer Prompt

Spend time in prayer, offering a heartfelt prayer of thanks to God for His faithfulness throughout this entire year. Confess any areas where you fell short and ask for His grace for the future. Pray for wisdom, clarity, and a deeper walk with Him in the year to come, surrendering your plans to His perfect will.

Personal Reflection & Growth Journal

Significant Moments / Insights from This Week's Study

What happened? What was the insight?

_____

_____

_____

_____

Emotional/Spiritual Responses:

_____

_____

_____

Spiritual Insights/Lessons Learned:

- First thoughts:

_____

_____

_____

_____

- New perspectives gained:

_____

_____

_____

_____

- My Response/Action:

_____

_____

_____

_____

What helped me connect with God/grow this ?week?

_____

_____

_____

_____

What hindered my connection/?growth?

_____

_____

_____

_____

Conclusion: A Journey of Faith, Growth, and Purpose

As we draw this year-long devotional journey to a close, we stand at a threshold, looking back at the ground we've covered and forward to the path ahead. It has been a privilege to walk through the foundational truths of God's character, the practical expressions of our faith, the richness of our connections with others, and the profound calling to live a life of purpose.

This guide was designed not just for reading, but for *living*. We've explored how a deeper understanding of **God's nature** (Quarter 1) transforms our worship, our trust, and our very identity. We then moved into **living out our faith** (Quarter 2), tackling practical applications in areas like forgiveness, patience, and managing our thoughts and words. Our journey continued into **connecting with others** (Quarter 3), emphasizing the beauty and challenge of community, relationships, and extending grace. Finally, we delved into **living with purpose** (Quarter 4), understanding our unique calling, stewarding our gifts, and leaving a godly legacy.

The true fruit of this journey lies not just in the pages filled, but in the heart transformed. It's in the quiet moments of prayer where God spoke, the challenging situations where you chose to act in faith, the relationships that deepened, and the new ways you discovered to serve.

Remember, the spiritual life is a continuous unfolding. The God who faithfully guided you through these 52 weeks is the same God who promises to be with you always, teaching, equipping, and empowering you for every step of your ongoing journey. May the insights gained, the habits formed, and the truths embraced become deeply embedded in your life, propelling you forward with greater **wisdom, love, and purpose**.

As you step into what lies ahead, carry with you the assurance that you are deeply loved, uniquely gifted, and eternally purposed by the Living God. Continue to seek His face, listen for His voice, and walk in obedience, knowing that His plan for you is good, perfect, and will bring Him glory.

May your life be a testament to His faithfulness.

Journal Pages

JOURNAL

JOURNAL

JOURNAL

JOURNAL

JOURNAL

Check out another book in the series

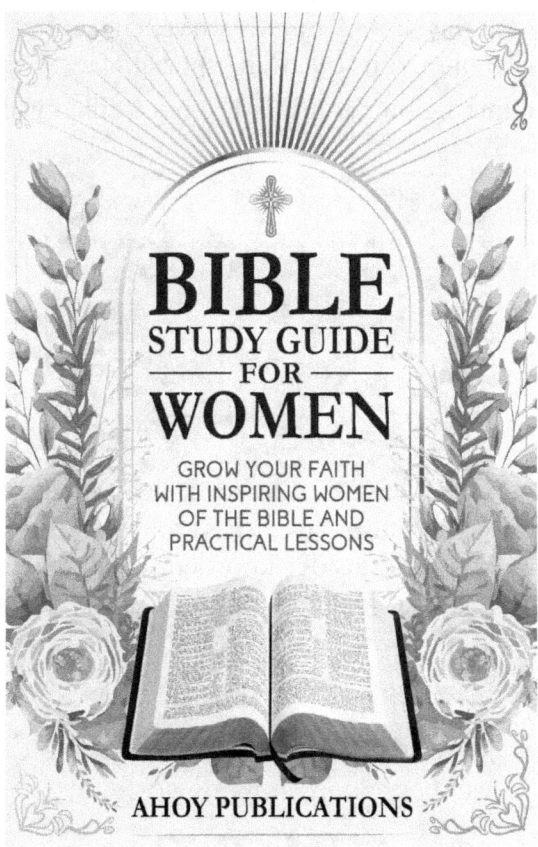

Welcome Aboard, Check Out This Limited-Time Free Bonus!

Ahoy, reader! Welcome to the Ahoy Publications family, and thanks for snagging a copy of this book! Since you've chosen to join us on this journey, we'd like to offer you something special.

Check out the link below for a FREE e-book filled with delightful facts about American History.

But that's not all - you'll also have access to our exclusive email list with even more free e-books and insider knowledge. Well, what are ye waiting for? Click the link below to join and set sail toward exciting adventures in American History.

Access your bonus here

https://ahoypublications.com/

Or, Scan the QR code!

www.ingramcontent.com/pod-product-compliance
Lightning Source LLC
Chambersburg PA
CBHW061728120626
46550CB00005B/1740